THE PERFECT COUNSELLING MANUAL

A Universal Approach to Counselling

By JJ James

The Perfect Counselling Manual

theperfectcounsel@gmail.com

Acknowledgement

With the highest gratitude and deepest appreciation, I thank my uncle A. A. James and my father E. E. James for their years of commitment to my welfare and advancement. Their sacrifices have made me who I am. To my educators, particularly, Rev. Dr Carmen Del Zotto, Rev. Dr Clarence Duff, Rev. Dr Frederick Wilson, Rev. Dr Jeff Yaneff and Rev. Dr Rondo Thomas, thank you for fanning the fire in my soul and equipping me for the work of God. As we know, no man is an island, and no man stands alone; with this, I want to say thank you to my friends, particularly Rev. Orlando Rowe, Evangelist Yvonne Reid, Rev. Maleke Adams, Minister Courtney Whitter and Minister Tesha Forrester, for your encouragement and support; God bless you. Speaking of friends, with the greatest gratitude and humility, I thank my beloved wife Victoria, without whom this book would not have been possible. Like true proverbs 31 women, she manages our home with excellence, affording me the luxury of producing a book. May God's blessing upon your life be spoken of. Finally, I want to say thank you to my lifelong cheerleader and beloved mother, Yvonne Magnus; I love you. Above all, I thank almighty God in whom I live and move and have my being, for His love and wisdom.

Dedication

This book is dedicated to those who are struggling to navigate their way through life; to those who seek transformation, healing and well-being; to the soldiers of the Kingdom of God, who are on the battlefield for the souls of men and to those who delight in the Word of God. To my children, Jahdai, Jesaiah and Joshua, may you find in me the contents of this book and may it never depart from your household; this is an inheritance. Finally, I dedicate this book to those who oppose the work and Word of the living God; here is the truth.

This book will change you!

For the word of God is quick, and powerful, and sharper than any two-edged sword, piercing even to the dividing asunder of soul and spirit, and of the joints and marrow, and is a discerner of the thoughts and intents of the heart.

(Hebrew 4:12).

Table of Contents

Introduction

After 200 years of practice, the world of psychiatry and counselling psychology have yet to provide a reliable, consistent system for healing those who suffer from various psychological and social issues. Until now, the leaders in the counselling and psychology industries have yet to agree upon proven strategies or solutions that therapists and patients can be confident in; as a result, it is practically impossible to find counsellors who agree upon methodology, theory, diagnosis or prognosis. Moreover, the *Diagnostic and Statistical Manual of Mental Disorders (DSM;* the bible for mental health professionals) is constantly changing; unstable in all its way's.

In many cases, the updated versions are void of disorders that existed in previous editions, while new disorders are added. The problem with this manual is that it is not exclusively based upon scientific research; rather, it is based upon the wavering opinion of so-called experts heavily influenced by political agendas. For example, in 1968, the DSM-11 listed homosexuality as a mental disorder; subsequently, various methods were employed to cure it. By 1987 however, this 'disorder' was completely removed. Now the question is, why was it in the book in the first place and why was it then removed? What scientific research was conducted to justify such actions? Believe it or not, it was decided upon with a simple vote by psychiatrists who attended the 1973 American Psychological Association convention. Imagine, all it took was a vote to determine the legitimacy of a so-called mental disorder. What if the same method was applied to cancer or diabetes?

If the guidebook used by mental health professionals is not based on proven facts, how can it be trusted to diagnose and treat patients with legitimate issues? Many patients, report being given a different diagnosis by every mental health professional they see which only complicates their original problem. This comes as no surprise because the body of knowledge available to mental health professionals is a collage of conflicting theories and philosophies from numerous psychologists. Consequently, each counsellor has to sift through the maze of theories, methods and approaches to create the perfect counselling recipe for each case and client.

Amidst this confusion, the counselling world is increasingly becoming more a reputable field of inquiry, demanding lengthy studies and training to practice. This poses another problem because every school's curriculum is unique; subsequently, there are countless institutions that mental health professionals must subscribe to for certification and governance. The problem is, each organisation has its own certification process, rules, standards and requirements. In Canada, there are over one hundred of these organisations. This counselling confusion has caused many people who practiced counselling effectively to lose confidence in their ability. Perhaps pastoral counsellors are the ones most overwhelmed and intimidated by the winds of psychology and psychiatry that have filled the atmosphere everywhere, causing them to lose confidence in their ability to counsel, and the use of the Bible. These ministers genuinely want to help their people, but they are uncertain about which program to pursue, which theory is best and how to balance it all with their religious convictions. Sadly, when all is said and done, the efforts of the counselling community are not as fruitful as some would have us believe. Many clients get worse during treatment, some are not helped at all, some feel better but are never wholly cured, fixed or healed; therefore, they are perpetually seeing a counsellor. To add insult to injury, counselling is also expensive.

When patients spend their money to see a counsellor, they expect solutions. We cannot ignore the fact that drugs seem to be the best thing that counselling and psychiatry have to offer today. However, clients are not interested in being used as guinea pigs, nor are they interested in medications with side effects worse than their original problem. Counselees need assurance that when they see a professional, there will be results. It means then that mental health professionals need a universal and reliable framework, if not hard and fast solutions, that they can build problem-solving programs and interventions upon. There needs to be a system with a single voice of authority that is always guaranteed to work. This will eliminate confusion, thereby making the industry more reputable and reliable.

Where do we go from here? Since the goal of counselling is to enhance human well-being by aligning counselees with what is good, right and healthy, we must begin the process by first asking two fundamental questions, "What is Man?" and "What is Truth?". Without the answers to these questions, counselling cannot be effective and fruitful. It goes without saying that you cannot fix something unless you first know what it is, what is its purpose and what it looks like when it is working properly. Unfortunately, if we were to ask these two questions to the majority of mental health professionals, the responses would vary across the board. Sigmund Freud who is credited as the father of psychoanalysis and has possibly contributed the most to the body of knowledge that secular counsellors rely on, had this to say about humanity in his letter to Oscar Pfister:

> *I have found little that is 'good' about human beings on the whole. In my experience, most of them are trash, no matter whether they publicly subscribe to this or that ethical doctrine or to none at all. That is something that you cannot say aloud, or perhaps even think* (Freud, 1918).

This man is revered, studied and followed, as a great teacher of psychology, yet his thoughts about human beings are anything but flattering. Clearly, there is a need for a shift in thinking. It is now time for the idols of the mental health industry to be overturned, for confusion to be dispelled and deception exposed, that truth may prevail.

I am suggesting that we go back to the beginning; back to where the original study of the psyche began. I propose to you now that the questions, "What is Man?" and "What is Truth?" Are philosophical questions that must be answered theologically. God created man; therefore, He is the most knowledgeable about him. Long before the so-called father of modern psychology, Wilhelm Wundt, built the first psychology laboratory at the University of Leipzig in 1879, the Bible was the original source of psychology and wisdom for daily living. Today, the Bible is known as an ancient religious book; hence, secular counsellors have no place for it in their work. They claim that the Bible does not and cannot address the complex issues of modern man, especially the new mental disorders that so-called experts have proposed. We will see in this book, however, that the Bible is timeless; it has never been revised or updated, yet it remains sharply relevant today. It is still effective and reliable for solving human problems; whether cognitive, spiritual, emotional, relational or moral in nature. It contains systems of morals, wisdom, instructions and spiritual insights that have governed nations and made simple men great. Throughout the ages, it has tamed vile men, purified corrupt men, and made insane men sane; it has saved marriages, united families, made poor men rich and rich men generous. Needless to say, those who want to help people live a victorious life must search the Scriptures for the truth about life and humanity.

The Bible introduces us to the Messiah, Jesus, who is called the "Wonderful Counsellor". He is credited as the one who has contributed the most to our understanding of humanity; more than any ancient philosopher or modern psychologist. He counsels His people personally, by His Spirit, with His Word, and through His ministers (counsellors). He is indeed the true counsellor. Who else would make the perfect counsellor but the one who is himself perfect? Upon His foundation, Biblical Counsellors build their counselling ministry that ultimately gives and changes lives. Biblical Counsellors are Christian Counsellors who use only the Bible in counselling. The American Association of Christian Counsellors, Psychologist Joshua Hook, research done by E. L. Worthington, and books like Bondage Breaker by Neil T. Anderson, and Counselling the Hard Cases by Stuart Scott and Heath Lambert, among others, all show that Biblical Counsellors are successfully helping their clients solve, heal and overcome their issues within a significantly faster time than secular counsellors. It is now becoming more and more popular with secular mental health professionals to bring their clients to Pastoral or Biblical counsellors out of desperation; this has proven to be effective (Anderson, 2000). One of the issues discussed in this book is the reality that secular counsellors generally blame physical causes (brain/body) for almost all so-called "mental illness" and behavioural issues; therefore, they constantly prescribe medication, even for someone who is grieving the death of a loved one. The Bible, however, goes far beyond the brain in its diagnosis of psychological, behavioural and relational problems. Those who carefully study the Bible have found a wealth of knowledge that can be classified as anthropology, psychology and sociology; all of which are necessary to understand the complexity of humanity. That being said, I declare to you that the author, the content and the goal of the Bible makes it the perfect counselling manual, far superior to any other. This book will demonstrate just that.

In the end, this book will show counsellors and counselees that there is an approach to counselling that is approved by God, that there is an authoritative, reliable and consistent voice in solving human problems. This is the voice that all counsellors need to be confident and effective. If you are a person having difficulties in life, whether they are of a psychological, spiritual or social nature, this book will help you navigate your way out. Biblical counsellors will appreciate this book because it will serve as a rational defence for why they choose the biblical way. Secular Counsellors will gain a new perspective of the Bible, a new view of humanity, reasons to reconsider their methods and a new counselling resource to turn to. Overall, counselling students, teachers and all those involved in the work of counselling will be challenged and sharpened by this material. Most of all, this book will change your heart and bring you closer to God, without whom no true counselling can be done.

PART ONE
The Perfect Author

Every good book attains its credibility and value from its author. This is why people invest in books written by trustworthy experts. On that note, to prove that the Bible is a competent counselling resource, the credibility of the author must be verified.

The author of the Bible is the God of Abraham and the God of Israel. He is also the God of King David (of Israel) and the God of the prophet Isaiah and the God of Jesus, the Messiah. He is the 'Most High' God who created the Heavens the Earth and all that dwells in it. He is void of sin, evil and unrighteousness; therefore, he cannot lie, deceive or be deceived. He is the expert of all experts; hence, He calls on men to seek Him. His name is YAHWEH-YESHUA. Let us now explore His character, authority and worldview to show that He is qualified to produce a perfect counselling manual.

CHAPTER 1
A Father and Friend

There is, "*one God, and father of all, who is above all, and through all, and in you all*" (Ephesians 4:6). These are the words of the great Apostle Paul, a man who had a remarkable supernatural encounter with God that completely changed his life. After his encounter, he developed such a profound and intimate relationship with God, that God was able to use him to produce half of the New Testament books of the Bible. Paul, a Jew of Jews, came to learn that the God of Israel is indeed, the ultimate universal Father of all. He is the same father that Jesus came to reveal to humanity; in fact, Jesus came to adopt humanity into the family of God (John 1:18; 14:6-10, Colossians 1:15, Ephesians 2:18-20). That being said, 'Father' is the most significant name of God disclosed in the Bible. It reveals to us that God is relational and wants to be known; He is not distant from humanity or beyond approach. The name father also indicates that we originate from God. This is the truth that many people lack; hence, their struggles with loneliness, identity, self-esteem, fear and personality issues. If only they knew who their true father really is.

He is Self-Existent and Eternal

We can know God to some degree through the observation of nature, the entire creation bears witness of Him. The greatest revelation of God, however, is found in the Bible and in Jesus who is the expressed image of God. We learn through Scripture that God is self-existent, meaning, He was not created; neither does He depend on anyone or anything to exist. He has no beginning or end; rather, He is the beginning and end (Isaiah 48:12-13, Revelation 1:8). People often ask, 'Where did God come from?' but they are never satisfied with the response that He is self-existent. In our limited human experience and understanding, everything in our reality seems to be based on cause and effect, ying and yang, one thing leading to another. However, we must accept that if God comes from something or someone else, then that thing or person is greater than God and is indeed God. God then, must be uncaused, considering that as God, He must be the cause of everything that exists. Furthermore, if we ask, 'Where did God come from?' we are assuming that time and space existed before God. This is contrary to Scripture which declares that God is Creator of all, including time and space (Genesis 1:1-5). Since God created time, He dwells outside of time, which makes Him eternal. Without a past or future, He dwells in the eternal now; reigning from everlasting to everlasting; His Kingdom has no end (Psalms 90:2, Isaiah 43:13). Because He is self-existent and eternal, by default, He is also self-sufficient, needing nothing and no one. God is a perfect being, without limitations; therefore, His counsel and ability to affect change must be superior to any other.

He is Holy

"*I am God, and not man; the Holy One in the midst of thee*," (Hosea 11:9). This one word 'holy' sets God apart from every other being. The word 'holy' informs us that God is morally perfect and separated from evil. The same cannot be said about me; neither can it be said about you; nevertheless, there is hope. God promises that one day those who believe and follow Him will be like Him (Romans 8:29, 1 John 3:2). The key thing here is that, if God is void of sin and evil, it means that He can do no wrong. This is important because the good moral standing of a counsellor is an essential quality; after all, a good counsellor is a model. It is difficult to perceive that a counselling resource written by an unethical, immoral person would help to promote quality of life, healthy relationships and psychological well-being. Likewise, it is difficult to perceive that an unethical, immoral or evil counsellor would be a good role model. God, on the other hand, is holy; therefore, He is qualified to call man into holiness. Man, after all, was made to be like God (Genesis 1:27, 1 Peter 1:15). We can agree that God's holy and moral perfection is reason enough to trust His counsel; certainly, the counsel of a perfect person is perfect.

He is Love

Greater than the revelation that the God of the Bible is the Father of the universe is the revelation that God is love. This is a peculiar statement because only this God of the Bible can make and defend such claims. The simple fact of the matter is that love is an action directed towards a particular object; therefore, for love to happen, there must be a giver and receiver. If this is true, how then can God declare that He is love, when He is only one person, and love requires at least two? This is where the uniqueness of Yahweh-Yeshua is displayed. The Bible shows that Yahweh is a triune God, three in one and one in three; God the Father, God the Son and God the Holy Spirit, united in a perfect relationship. Strauch (2003) describes the relationship this way, "Father, Son, and Holy Spirit exist in loving communal life with one another, speaking to one another, working together, giving and receiving, and delighting in each other for all eternity" (p. 266). He further states, "there has always existed an amazing, dynamic interrelationship between the Father, Son and Holy Spirit characterized by love; each member in the holy fellowship of the Godhead loves and is beloved" (p. 266). In simple terms, God is one community of lovers; hence, God is love. At the root of many counselling cases is a failure to give or receive love; consequently, love is vital in counselling.

God's love is undeserved, yet He holds nothing back. His love is displayed in the person of Jesus who sacrificed His life, that the whole world may be saved from the holy justified wrath of God (John 3:16). Although mankind rebelled against the Holy Father, He sent His Son to rescue those who want to escape the darkness of this evil, sinful, broken world that they may be free to live an abundant life that pleases God. "*Greater love hath no man than this that he lay down his life for his friends*" says Jesus (John 15:13). Yet not only His friends, for the Scriptures are clear that "*...when we were enemies (of God), we were reconciled to God by the death of his Son...*" (Romans 5:10). The Scripture shows that the depth of God's love is so deep, it is extending even unto His enemies.

He is the same yesterday, today and forever

> *"For I am the LORD, I change not; therefore ye sons of Jacob are not consumed"* (Malachi 3:6).

The design of human beings and the root cause of their problems change not; therefore, there is no sense in having a counselling resource that constantly changes its philosophy, methods, prognosis, diagnosis and definitions. An inconsistent counsellor or counselling resource is harmful to a client and detrimental to the therapeutic process. It is therefore essential to have a counsellor who is consistent in belief, behaviour and practice. Considering that consistency goes hand in hand with reliability, the author of the Bible is the most reliable source there is. He is the same yesterday, today and forever (Hebrews 13:8). He changes not; after all, He is perfect. He knows all things and has all power; therefore, he has no need to change. His impeccable unchanging character and unshakable love qualifies Him to produce a reliable counselling resource.

A Perfect Father

Yahweh is the creator of all that exists and is infinitely abundant. He provides for and sustains all of creation, supplying all their needs whether physical or spiritual. He is an unchanging father that loves perfectly; eternally good is He. Certainly, His fatherly qualities make Him a good counsellor.

A Friend

"Ointment and perfume rejoice the heart: so doth the sweetness of a man's friend by hearty counsel,"
(Proverbs 27:9).

Since we intend to know more about God's personality and character, it is important to consider His friendliness, it provides the context to understand His goodness, grace, kindness, and love. God has friends; in fact, He called Abraham, the father of Israel, His friend (Isaiah 41:8). Jesus also called His disciples friends; friends who He eventually died for (John 15:13-15). He was so friendly, He was accused of being a friend of sinners, which He was indeed. Because Jesus is the perfect image, representation and expression of God, we must consider His personality, character and teachings to get a better understanding of whom and how God is (Hebrew 1:1-3).

An examination of the Greek and Hebrew use of the word 'friend' in Scripture denotes a loving relationship void of sexuality and romance. It is a trusting relationship. It goes without saying that a friend by definition, is a good thing; nevertheless, some friends are better than others. We are concerned with the quality of friend God is. Churchill (1900) speaking about friendship with God wrote:

> *To come into friendship with God is really to share his life; but the very life of God is love, self-giving, pouring himself out into the life of his creatures. To share his life, therefore, is necessarily to enter into like loving relations to all men* (P. 559).

He is Good

"You know of Jesus of Nazareth, how God anointed Him with the Holy Spirit and with power, and how He went about doing good and healing all who were oppressed by the devil, for God was with Him" (Acts 10:38). God's goodness towards man began at creation and

never ended. The creation story in Genesis tells us that God made man the crown of creation, giving him dominion over all other created things. In fact, man is called God's masterpiece (Ephesians 2:10). It is obvious throughout the Bible that God has the welfare of humanity at heart and is actively helping man to enter a better experience of life (2 Peter 1:3). Scripture declares, "For the Lord God is a sun and shield: the Lord will give grace and glory, no good thing will he withhold from them that walk uprightly" (Psalm 84:11). Furthermore, *"take no thought, saying, what shall we eat? Or, what shall we drink? Or, wherewithal shall we be clothed? (For after all these things do the Gentiles seek) for your heavenly Father knoweth that ye have need of all these things"* (Mathew 6:31-32). God's goodness is clearly demonstrated in His kindness toward man.

It must be made clear however, that God is not good because of the good things He does; rather, He Himself is goodness, original, infinite goodness. Goodness is His nature; in fact, the entire creation is a natural expression of God's goodness. This explains the beauty of the world and its compatibility with human life. God Himself declared His creation good (Genesis 1-2). Although there are hundreds of passages of Scripture that shows God's kindness, gentleness and goodness, the matter of the goodness of God is simply this: God is goodness; therefore, all that comes from Him is good. All that He thinks, says and does is good. By nature, He cannot do or produce that which is not good because He is all goodness. All that is good is good because He made it so. The goodness of God is nothing but His infinite, holy, righteous benevolence towards His creation; but this is not just an act, it is the state of God's being. His goodness is simply beyond human comprehension; hence, it is better experienced than understood. King David of Israel embraced God's goodness in these words: "*How great is Thy goodness, which Thou hast stored up for those who fear Thee, which Thou hast wrought for those who take refuge in Thee, before the sons of men!*" (Psalms 31:19). God is the type of friend all people need in the times of trouble. The statement, "God is good" may be a modern-day cliché but it is certainly an ancient truth.

Many critics will be quick to say that the God of the Bible is not good because there are too many stories of gruesome killings in the Bible. However, God is an all-wise God of justice, righteousness and peace; therefore, if He orders the punishment of a people, it is His good, holy, righteous justice at work, whether we understand or not.

Full of Grace

"...But where sin abounded, grace did much more abound" (Romans 5:20). All men have sinned against God; subsequently, all men have become enemies of God, deserving of His wrath and punishment but God chose to forgive (Romans 5:10). Forgiveness means freedom from bondage and newness of life. God's grace is constantly calling men to receive this forgiveness. In fact, He has done everything to ensure that men will be saved; saved from all evil and His own punishment (Romans 5:9). The grace of God towards man was demonstrated in the crucifixion of Jesus Christ, who was punished by God instead of humanity. In other words, Jesus' death cancelled the debt that humanity owed to God because of their sins. His death has appeased the wrath of God; therefore, those who accept Jesus as God over their lives have peace with the heavenly father; they live without fear of divine punishment. Moreover, the death of Jesus has reunited man with God, and now, through faith in Jesus, man can have power over sin, sickness, death, oppression, depression, obsessions and evil spirits.

Ephesians 2 shows that when humanity made itself the enemy of God through disobedience, God willingly rescued His enemies from their sorrows and made them His friends; at least those who believe and accept Him. Certainly, a person who is kind and forgiving towards his enemies will be far more gracious towards his friends. Any individual, who is full of grace, not condemning or rejecting but forgiving, is an asset to one's success and well-being in life. God has shown Himself to be a friend that offers strong support, one that will move heaven and earth to help those He loves. These are qualities that a counselee needs in a counsellor.

Grace is defined by Merriam-Webster's Dictionary as, "A virtue coming from God; unmerited divine assistance given humans for their regeneration or sanctification; a state of sanctification enjoyed through divine assistance." In simple terms, grace is favour or assistance given to an undeserving person. It shows God's complete commitment to humanity. His desire is for men to live a righteous life of peace, joy and prosperity; this is what He offers His friends.

He is Faithful

"God is not a man that he should lie; neither the son of man that he should repent: hath he said, and shall he not do it? Or hath he spoken, and shall he not make it good?" (Numbers 23:19). Relationships are often faced with many challenges, but a breach of trust always taints a relationship, often destroying it. This reveals to us that faithfulness or trustworthiness is arguably the most important quality in a friendship. The author of the Bible has proven to be reliable, credible and faithful time and time again. He has never been unfaithful or unreliable throughout history, what he says he will do he has done. Indeed, the entire Bible is a testimony of God's faithfulness. King David of Israel testifies of this truth saying, *"I have been young, and now am old; yet have I not seen the righteous forsaken, nor his seed begging bread"* (Psalm 37:25).

The Bible is replete with promises and prophecies from the author who has never failed to fulfil. Infact, there are 2500 prophecies in the Bible, 2000 of which have already been fulfilled; the remaining 500 are scheduled for the future. A great example of God's faithfulness is seen in His prophecy of the Messiah, whom He promised would come to conquer Satan, the evil one and sin (Genesis 3:15). Four thousand years later, the Messiah comes and fulfils the prophecy (Colossian 2:15). Not only did He fulfil this prophecy from Genesis but also another 300 prophecies found in the Old Testament.

Another example of God's faithfulness is seen in His relationship with Abraham, the father of Israel, who God called His friend (James 2:23). Abraham stands as a testimony of the honesty, loyalty and reliability of God. The book of Genesis shows that God made several promises to Abraham, the highlight of which is found in chapter 12:1-3:

> *Now the LORD had said unto Abram, Get thee out of thy country, and from thy kindred, and from thy father's house, unto a land that I will shew thee: And I will make of thee a great nation, and I will bless thee, and make thy name great; and thou shalt be a blessing: And I will bless them that bless thee, and curse him that curseth thee: and in thee shall all families of the earth be blessed.*

This 5000-year-old promise is fulfilled and still being fulfilled. God blessed Abraham with great wealth and honour (Genesis 13). He was highly respected among his neighbours who called him a prince, even though he did not descend from royalty (Genesis 23:6). When God spoke this promise to Abraham, both he and his wife were very old and without children due to barrenness. Also, there was no land or people called Israel; however, Abraham eventually had sons. His barren wife even gave birth to her first son at 90 years old. Abraham became the grandfather of the Jacob whose name was later changed to Israel. He is the father of the twelve tribes of the nation of Israel. Today, Israel is a great and wealthy nation possessing its own land in the Middle East. Furthermore, Jews are seated in high places in every field, owning most of the media,

Hollywood, and Disney World, while making great contributions to the advancement of technology. According to Israel's most popular news website, ynetnews.com, "Jews make up less than half of one percent of the world's population, but they consistently have made up more than twenty percent of the Forbes 400 list of the world's richest people." God promised to bless them and make them great and He did.

God also promised Abraham that he would be the father of many nations. Today, Judaism, Christianity and Islam are the most dominant religions on earth with a population of about 4 billion collectively, and all three of them call Abraham their father. Abraham is also called the Father of faith (Romans 4:16). The Bible teaches that those who believe in God like Abraham will be counted as his children. This means that even those who are not related to Abraham by blood have the privilege to be his sons by faith, through the Spirit (Galatians 3:7). Most certainly this prophecy is still being fulfilled, considering that every Christian convert is indeed a son of Abraham by faith while every Jew is a son of Abraham by blood. This means that Abraham's descendants are still increasing upon the earth. God also promised to curse the enemies of Israel, and this is what happened to Egypt, Assyria and Babylon to name a few; all these nations fell from power and prestige after attacking Israel. God broke those nations, and until this day none of Israel's enemies has prevailed against them. The same is true for Christianity (sons of Abraham by faith) which has survived all attempts to destroy it for over two thousand years. God's faithfulness to Abraham continues today, even though Abraham is dead.

When it comes to the work of counselling, the integrity, character, empathy and psychological stability of the counsellor is crucial to the therapeutic process; after all, counsellors ought to be role models. The Author of the Bible has shown Himself to be a loving father and a gracious friend. He is full of compassion, kindness and faithfulness towards humanity. He is always doing all that is within His power to improve man's well-being. When we add this to His impeccable character and irreproachable morals, what is seen, are the qualities and attributes of a perfect father, counsellor and credible author for a counselling manual.

CHAPTER 2
His Authority & Worldview

If the author of the Bible is to be recognized as a credible source for counselling, His authority must be established. Experts and professionals in any field are an authority in some sense; hence, their point of views and advice are highly regarded, often demanding a monetary value. Counselees are often paying handsome fees and making significant life changes at the command of a counsellor because professional counsellors on all levels, by virtue of their function, are a voice of authority. We know that all authority must have a basis or source from which it is derived; therefore, the basis of the counsellor's authority must be considered. Secular counsellors derive their authority from their education, training and the professional bodies that endorse them. The author of the Bible however, has no such endorsement or training, so the question now is, where did He get His authority from?

Merriam-Webster's Dictionary gives the following definitions for the word authority: "a power to influence or command thought, opinion or behaviour." "Persons in command (specifically government) and a convincing force." Baker's Evangelical Dictionary, on the other hand, defines authority as, "the freedom to decide or a right to act without hindrance." If all authority must have a basis or source from which it is derived, what then is the basis of God's authority? Many would quickly argue that since God is the all-knowing, all-powerful Creator of the universe, naturally, He has the right to rule over it. Although this is true, it is not sufficient to make God a moral authority and a beneficial source for human well-being and development. In other words, if the creator was all-knowing and all-powerful but morally corrupt or evil, man could not look to Him as an authoritative source for solution and guidance. This shows that the basis of God's authority cannot rest upon the fact that He is the omnipotent and omniscient creator of the world. Rather, the true basis of God's authority is His perfect character and nature. In other words, God is the authoritative source for human well-being because He is a perfect person. This means, He knows the way to wholeness. Consider this, If Yahweh was not the creator and was not all-knowing and all-powerful, He would still be the authoritative source for human well-being, because He is well-being.

God is Authority

In truth, authority is a biblical concept, not a secular one; as a matter of fact, the reason there are so many different forms of government today is due to the distortion of what the Bible teaches about authority. The Bible shows that there is no authority except that which God has ordained and established (Romans 13:1). In other words, Yahweh-Yeshua is the originator of the very concept of authority. Mayhue (2004) states:

> *God did not inherit His authority--there was no one to bequeath it to Him. God did not receive His authority--there was no one to bestow it on Him. God's authority did not come by way of an election--there was no one to vote for Him. God did not seize His authority--there was no one to steal it from. God did not earn His authority--it was already His. God inherently embodies authority because He is the great "I AM"* (Exodus 3:14; John 8:58) (p. 228).

Considering that the self-existent, eternal Creator alone is completely perfect, holy and without blame, possessing all knowledge and power, we conclude that He does not have authority but that He is authority; original authority. He alone has absolute freedom to do as He pleases and absolute power to influence thought and behaviour.

Perfect Authority

When God introduced Himself to Moses as the "*I AM*," it is as though He was saying to Moses, 'I am absolute; absolutely perfect.' Moses later declared, "*He is the Rock, his work is perfect: for all his ways are judgement: a God of truth and without iniquity, just and right is he*" (Deuteronomy 32:4). God is not just authority but good and righteous authority. His authority is never exercised to control and manipulate, but to love and redeem. This is demonstrated in His decision to judge and recreate the world in the blessed Christ (Constantineanu, 2010, p. 19). His intention toward humanity is wholly good. His plan is to give us hope, and life in abundance (Jeremiah 29:11; John 10:10). Jesus, who is God incarnate declares, "*follow me, I am the way the truth and the life*" (Matthew 16:24; John 14:6). He is the path to righteousness, perfection of character and well-being. Since He is perfect in nature, morality and character, possessing all knowledge and power, there is no conceivable problem in the universe that He cannot make right. Additionally, there is no reason for man to not trust Him. He has shown throughout history and in the Scripture, that He is the qualified authority on all matters. By default, Yahweh-Yeshua is ultimate authority and a perfect problem solver.

Finally, the authority of God and the authority of Scripture are knit together. This idea is supported by John 1:1, "*In the beginning was the Word, and the Word was with God, and the Word was God.*" The phrase, "*the Word was God*" makes it clear that there is no separation between God and His Word. The point here is that the Bible which is the Word of God, gets its authority from God, the ultimate authority. In simple terms, the Bible is authoritative because it carries and expresses the will of God. On that note, men should honour the Scripture and use it as an authoritative guide to life and godliness.

His Worldview

A worldview is one's fundamental convictions and basic beliefs about the world. Every conscious person has a worldview; furthermore, every counsellor has a set of presuppositions that shape both the way he approaches counselling and the goal he hopes to achieve in counselling. Since we are interested in the kind of person and counsellor the author of the Bible is, we must examine His worldview. We are particularly interested in what the author of Scripture thinks about deity, creation, the problem of evil, humanity and the meaning of life.

On Deity and Creation

The author of the Bible declares that Yeshua (Jesus of Nazareth), the son of Mary and descendant of King David, is the Creator, Ruler and Redeemer of the universe (Isaiah 9:6, Matthew 28:18). He is designated, King of kings and the Lord of lords (Revelation 19:15-16). In Him dwells the entire Godhead (Colossians 2:9), which is, God the Father, God the Son and God the Holy Spirit. Nevertheless, there are not three Gods but one. John 1:1-4, 14 makes it very clear that the God and Creator of the universe came to the Earth in the form of a man and was recognized as the Son of God; hence his name, Emmanuel which means 'God with us'- God on earth with man. The Bible is unapologetic about the fact that Jesus created the universe and all that is in it, to express His glory (Psalm 19:1, Romans 1:20). In short, Yeshua is the God and Saviour of the world, as far as the author of Scripture is concerned.

A word to those who say they believe in God but not Jesus:
"For unto us a child is born, unto us a son is given: and the government shall be upon his shoulder: and his name shall be called Wonderful, Counsellor, The mighty God, The everlasting Father, The Prince of Peace" (Isaiah 9:6).

This prophecy came about eight hundred years before the birth of Jesus, and it speaks of no other but the son of Mary. It clearly states that he is the mighty God, The everlasting Father and Prince of Peace. Other Scriptures on this topic to reference are (Mathew 1:23, John 1, Hebrews 8).

Evil's Origin

All people at some point in life wrestle with the presence of evil in the world, Philosophers and theologians are no exception; they have grappled for centuries over the conflict of a good God and an evil world. Many have sought to provide some rational argument to settle the matter. Some have concluded that there is no God; others, that God is not good, while some believe that God is good, but He is weak and powerless in the face of evil. The real quest, however, is to investigate what God Himself says about the matter of evil. Let us first look at some definitions for evil. Unger's Bible Dictionary says: "evil is the comprehensive term under which are included all disturbances of the divinely appointed harmony of the universe." Unger's further divides evil into two categories: physical evil (a disorder in the physical world) and moral evil (a disorder in the moral world). Disorder in the moral world is a sophisticated way of saying sin and unrighteousness. Alan Richardson's Theological Word Book of the Bible defines evil as, "anything that causes pain, unhappiness or misery including the discipline of punishment sent by God".

Now that evil is defined, we are interested in how it came to be. In Matthew 13:19, 39, Jesus speaks of one who steals or distorts the Word of God that people receive. Jesus refers to this person as the '*Wicked One*' and the '*Devil.*' Again, in John 8:44, Jesus speaks of this devil, referring to him as the '*Father of Lies*' and '*a murderer from the beginning.*' Interestingly, Jesus, in John 12:30 and the Apostle Paul, in 2 Corinthians 4:4, ascribes the title "*Prince and God of this age*," to the same devil. In Luke 4:6-8 this devil is called "*Satan.*" Revelation 12:7-9 shows that this devil called Satan was evicted from heaven with his entourage of angels. It also shows that he is the same serpent that tempted Eve (Genesis 3). Now the idea and meaning behind the words, 'devil' and 'Satan' is, "*accuser, adversary and demon.*" Satan is the adversary of God and the accuser of man. 1 John 3:8 shows that Satan sinned from the beginning and that all who remain sinners are of him; this shows that Satan is the original sinner and originator of sin. He is the one that disturbed the divinely ordered harmony of the universe causing the whole creation pain and misery. Isaiah 14 and Ezekiel 28 give's a bit of his biography. We are told that he is a created being of the angelic order; a cherub, made perfect in all his ways. He was full of beauty and wisdom, dwelling in the holy mountain of God. Eventually, his own beauty and splendour made him proud, filling his heart with the lofty and evil imagination that he could replace God. This motivated him to rebel against God and to initiate treason in heaven. This resulted in a war in heaven, and he was thrown out. Genesis 3 shows this serpent at work, trying to lead man in a rebellion against God, as he himself had done; unfortunately, the serpent was successful. He led man into disobedience and sin entered the human race. Satan then, is the presence of evil in the world according to the author of the Bible (God).

The Effect of Evil

According to Genesis 3:17-18 and Romans 8:22, the entire creation was affected by the entrance of sin in the world. Satan's rebellion introduced darkness in the universe; physical darkness on earth and moral darkness upon man (Genesis 1:2; 6:5). The result is that the Earth was cursed; thorns and thistles came as a result, and the animals became hostile towards man. Sin took man's innocence, gave him the knowledge of good and evil and filled him with guilt (Genesis 3:5-8). Sin corrupted man and introduced death (Romans 6:23, Genesis 2:17). Death came on two levels; physical death and spiritual death. Man needs God, the source of his life to live;

therefore, spiritual death is defined as separation from God. This spiritual death further subjected the human body to perversion, weakness, sickness and the physical death of the body. Man's mental faculties and emotions were also negatively affected; they were turned away from God.

Sin is also hereditary (Romans 5:19, Romans 3:23, Psalm 51:5). The nature of sin and death that entered the first man Adam, corrupted his seed. This corruption was passed on to his children from generation to generation; therefore, all men are born with the proclivity to sin. The Westminster Confession of Faith expresses this truth; "All mankind, by their fall, lost communion with God, are under his wrath and curse, and so made liable to all miseries in this life, to death itself, and to the pains of hell forever." We conclude here that sin is the universal problem which has thrown the entire creation into opposition with its creator and ruler, resulting in discord, wickedness, pain and misery; this is the view of the author of Scripture.

God's Response to Evil

"For the eyes of the Lord are over the righteous, and his ears are open unto their prayers: but the face of the Lord is against them that do evil" (1 Peter 3:12). Frankly speaking, God hates sin, and the Scripture is very vocal about this (Psalm 7:11, 2 Thessalonians 2:12, Revelation 20:15). Many individuals and nations throughout history have been punished severely by God for their acts of sin. God hates sin so much that His whole plan of redemption includes the total eradication of sin from the universe. This was the mission of God incarnate, Jesus the Christ (1 John 3:8). He came that man may have power over sin and evil, that they be filled with joy, peace, love, righteousness and life more abundantly. In other words, He came to give man freedom from sin and its effects. Jesus also promises that a day will come when the devil shall be destroyed, evil eradicated and a new heaven and earth, void of sin and evil, shall be

established. (Romans 14:17, Romans15:13, 2 Peter 3:13, Revelation 19:20). In the meantime, God has given man all that he needs for life and Godliness (2 Peter 1:3); of course, all that men need is the Gospel of Jesus and the Holy Spirit. The Saviour of the world, the Lamb of God, is God's remedy for sin, for him who believes. He is the one that saves the world from the power of Satan, evil, darkness and sin (Colossians 1:13, Acts 16:31). He is the great warrior that destroys evil in the world. We conclude then that God sees evil as a temporary thing and that Jesus is the ever-present solution for evil in the world.

The Purpose of Evil

A note must be made here about the sovereignty of God and its implications upon the presence of evil in the world. Many people ask, "if God is the sovereign, loving, all-powerful King, who rules over all, why does He still allow evil to have reigned, including natural disasters? According to King Solomon, "*The LORD has made everything for its own purpose, even the wicked for the day of evil*" (Proverbs 16:4). God allows evil to aid in the fulfilment of His purpose; however, He does not create or participate in evil. Evil is diabolically contrary to Him. He is eternal goodness, love and Holiness, no evil is in Him or comes from Him. Rather, the angels of God and the sons of God (humanity) who rebelled against Him, and continues to rebel even until now, are the ones responsible for creating and perpetuating evil. Men and fallen angels, day after day with their free will choose to turn away from God and from what is good and right. With their free will, they choose immorality and by doing so create evil; evil then begets evil. The sovereignty of God only allows evil to highlight the goodness of God. The Bible shows that when the creation turned away from God by its own free will, God Almighty responded with the power of His love, to deliver it from its fallen, broken and corrupt state. God showed His disapproval of evil by implementing a redemption plan, a war plan, a restoration plan, and a victory plan, led by Jesus Christ. In the face of evil and offence, God took the opportunity to display His love, power, glory and grace.

A classic example of God's sovereignty and goodness at work in the mist of evil is the story of the young man Joseph (Genesis 37-50). This young man was sold into slavery by his jealous, egotistic brothers. He later ended up in prison in Egypt after being wrongfully accused of sexual assault. This son of Jacob encounters trouble after trouble from the time his brothers scolded and sold him. Nevertheless, God was behind the scenes working out every unfortunate thing in his favour. Joseph had the gift to interpret dreams, which he did for two men while he was in prison. In due time, the Pharaoh needed a dream interpreter aswell, and one of those men told the Pharaoh about Joseph. Joseph interpret the Pharaoh's dream and he was so impressed with Joseph's wisdom and character, he made Joseph a ruler in Egypt.

Now, God did not put evil in Joseph's brother's hearts, nor did God tell the woman to wrongfully accuse him, but God did give him the gift and wisdom to interpret dreams. God also created the opportunity for him to meet the Pharaoh. The significance of this is the fact that, Egypt became a haven for the Jews in the time of famine because a Jew was ruler in Egypt. Here we see that God does not create or perform evil; rather, while men and demons are doing evil, God is behind the scenes working on behalf of His righteous people; allowing everything, good and bad, to serve His good purpose. In short, God does not do evil but He allows it to help in fulfil His will. This is comforting to the person who is facing unexplainable difficulties in life. If that person will trust in God and live for Him, they can have the assurance that their unwanted experiences will work out to be a blessing. However, those who do not subscribe to the God of the Bible cannot have this assurance. This may sound arrogant, but logically speaking, these teachings and promises are from the God of Scripture alone. Furthermore, His commitment and promises are only for those who follow Him; therefore, the man who refuses to follow God cannot say that the unfortunate things in his life are going to be a blessing.

The Author's (of the Bible) view of Man

Man is God's masterpiece; the image and the glory of God, made to rule over God's creations (Genesis 1:28, Psalm 8:6, 1Corinthians 11:7, Ephesians 2:10). He was intentionally fashioned in the hands of God and is in no way the product of evolution or chance. God's own image and likeness is the template for his makeup and design. He consists of two main parts; the material and immaterial. The material is the body and the immaterial is the soul/spirit; both are made by God (Genesis 2:7). The body is made from the soil of the earth, and the soul/spirit comes directly from God himself (Job 33:4).

Man is a moral being; he has the ability to know right and wrong and to choose between them (Joshua 24:14-15). Since he was created to rule and to represent God, necessarily he is endowed with intelligence, imagination, the ability to reason and the free will to choose and to act; this makes him a rational being (Isaiah 1:18, Matthew 16:7). Man is also a being of love; he was made by love, for love and to reciprocate love, without which he is void and empty. In summary, man is a moral, rational, relational being who is dependent on God for his life (Acts 17:23-31).

Man is not a product that randomly (by chance) evolved from primates, as evolution teaches. If that were true, then man would have no dignity or meaning in life. Ultimately, it would not matter if we treated people like trash. It would not matter if the rich took advantage of the poor, or the strong oppressed the weak. After all, evolution teaches "the survival of the fittest." But the Bible teaches that man is a special creation of God, and as such, he has dignity and meaning in life. He was created for God's glory, to be God's vice-regent, and to have dominion over the earth (Gonzales, 2008, p.86). Subsequently, man is required to treat each other with honour.

The Purpose of the Universe and Life

God made all things for Himself as the natural expression of His being and glory; therefore, the whole purpose of life and the Universe is to manifest the love, power, glory and character of God in all things everywhere for eternity. The apostle Paul declares that Jesus:

> *Who is the image of the invisible God, the firstborn of every creature: For by him were all things created, that are in heaven, and that are in earth, visible and invisible, whether they be thrones, or dominions, or principalities, or powers: all things were created by him, and for him: And he is before all things, and by him all things consist. And he is the head of the body, the church: who is the beginning, the firstborn from the dead; that in all things he might have the pre-eminence. For it pleased the Father that in him should all fullness dwell...* (Colossians 1:15-19).

Seeing that I am not as wise and eloquent as Apostle Paul, in simple terms what he is saying is that, the whole universe came in to being both to glorify Jesus and to display His glory.

The eternal reality of the universe is about the love story within the Godhead (Father, Son and Holy Spirit). According to the author of Scripture, the Father of the universe is so pleased with His Son, He gave Him all authority, power, dominion and rule over all of creation (Matthew 17:5; 28:18, Hebrew 1:4-10). Man finds himself in the middle of this love exchange as a gift; a bride (followers of Jesus) to be exact, from the Father to the Son (Revelation 21:9, Ephesians 5:25-32). This bride will be made one with her Groom, sharing in His kingdom, glory and power. The Son, who is also bent on glorifying His Father through loving obedience, is committed to the well-being of His bride; committed to present her worthy before His Father for eternity. In the end, better yet, for eternity, the love, glory, beauty and power of God are expressed everywhere in all things; all because it pleases God (Ephesians (1:5-9, Philippians 2:13). This is the meaning and purpose of life according to the author of Scripture. Here concludes the worldview of the author of the Bible.

He is Competent

Why is the Bible relevant for counselling you ask? Because YAHWEH –YESHUA, the God and author of the Bible is holy, all knowing, all powerful, self-sufficient and perfect in nature. He is the creator of all living things; the sustainer of life. He is strength, hope, life and love. He is a father to the fatherless; a friend to the unloved, an expert on life and humanity. In Him we live, move and have our being (Acts 17:28). He knows every heart because every soul is in His hands; therefore, His diagnosis and prognosis are specific and sharp. His passion for man's healing, comfort, deliverance and victory is unmatched. Now if the counsel of imperfect, sinful men, like Sigmund Freud, Adler, Rogers and Jung are praised, despite their limited knowledge and tainted character, then certainly the counsel of the Holy, loving, omniscient Father of the universe is relevant and should be sought after by all men, at all cost, at all times.

Part Two
The Perfect Content

Human beings, their reality and problems are complex; needless to say, the work of counselling is also complex, drawing upon different disciplines and diverse knowledge to help counselees. Understandably, it may be difficult to see at a glance how the content of Scripture is relevant to counselling and psychology. However, a careful study of the Bible will reveal that it is replete with history, anthropology, psychology, sociology and wisdom for daily living. This section of the book will explore the vastness of the content of the Bible, to show that it provides adequate knowledge and insights for effective and holistic counselling.

CHAPTER 3
What is Man?

No one can fix the unknown; a good grasp of anthropology then, which is simply the study of human beings, is necessary for effective counselling. These next two chapters will explore the Scripture for its insights about the human design and its relevance to counselling.

The Origin of Man

And the LORD God formed man of the dust of the ground and breathed into his nostrils the breath of life; and man became a living soul (Genesis 2:7).

But from the beginning of the creation God made them male and female (Mark 10:6).

The Bible declares that man was made by God. The unique thing about this claim is that the Bible is more than just one book; it is a collection of sixty-six books, penned by forty different men working independently. All these writers, without consulting each other, agree that the creator of the Earth also made Man. The apostle Paul declares:

God that made the world and all things therein, seeing that he is Lord of heaven and earth, dwelleth not in temples made with hands; Neither is worshipped with men's hands, as though he needed anything, seeing he giveth to all life, and breath, and all things; And hath made of one blood all nations of men for to dwell on all the face of the earth, and hath determined the times before appointed, and the bounds of their habitation; That they should seek the Lord, if haply they might feel after him, and find him, though he be not far from every one of us: For in him we live, and move, and have our being; as certain also of your own poets have said, For we are also his offspring. Forasmuch then as we are the offspring of God, we ought not to think that the Godhead is like unto gold, or silver, or stone, graven by art and man's device (Acts 17:24-29).

What is particularly unique about this statement is that it is found in the book of Acts, which is written by Doctor Luke. "Luke is a historian of the first rank; not merely are his statements of fact trustworthy; this author should be placed along with the very greatest of historians. . .", according to atheist historian and archaeologist William Ramsay (Ramsay, 1953). Ramsay was a radical unbeliever who like many others, disregarded the claims of the Bible, deeming them fictional. To prove the Bible false, Ramsay relocated to the Middle East to conduct his research. After combing through the records of history and the findings of archaeology; Ramsay, the son of an atheist and atheist himself, found no grounds to disprove the Book of Acts. He rather found evidence to confirm its accuracy and authenticity. In the end, Ramsay became a Christian, authoring many books about his discoveries. This fact is important because it testifies to the reality that the Bible is not a religious book containing mythological ideas. It is a book of facts and truth; therefore, statements like, "*we are also his offspring,*" should be taken seriously. God also confirms through His prophet Isaiah that He is the creator of man; "*I have made the earth, and created man upon it: I, even my hands, have stretched out the heavens, and all their host have I commanded*" (Isaiah 45:12). The point here is that man originated from God; therefore, God is father; man is son.

The Nature of Man

Now that we have established that the creator of the universe made man, we will further look at man's design. According to Genesis 2:7, man is made from the dust of the earth, which forms his physical body, and from the '*breath of life*' which God blew into the body. These two parts form the whole human being- a *living soul.* The Bible teaches then that humans are made up of two parts, the material (physical body) and immaterial (spirit). There are several views and debates over the distinction and definition of soul and spirit; however, much of the confusion came about because of the mixing of Greek philosophies and biblical doctrines in the early days of the church. Greek philosophers taught that there is a substance called 'spirit' that unites the body and soul; hence, the popular idea that man is made up of three parts; soul, spirit, and body. In any case, when the Scripture speaks for itself, soul and spirit are not two different things. The terms are rather used interchangeably throughout the Bible, in the same way the words 'Scripture' and 'Bible' are used in this book. Both words are used in the same way throughout Scripture, to convey the same ideas. Some scholars argue that the 'spirit' is the God-conscious part of the human being, while the 'soul' is the general animal life within the body; however, the Bible does not concretely support this idea. For a better understanding, let us consider the definition and biblical use of these terms. The first part of the Bible (Old Testament) is originally written in Hebrew, the second part in Greek (New Testament); it is therefore necessary to examine both languages.

Soul

The Hebrew word for Soul is - 'Nephesh'- meaning: "a breathing creature; the man himself; the seat of emotions, passions and appetite; the activity of the character" (Strong's Dictionary). 'Nephesh'- is used to refer to the whole inner nature of man and his personality (Unger's Bible Dictionary).

The Greek word for Soul is - 'Psuche' (pronounced: sookay) - meaning: "breath; a living being; the vital force which animates the body; the seat of feelings, desires, affections and aversions" (Strong's Dictionary).

Spirit

The Hebrew word for Spirit is - 'Ruwach' or 'Ruah' - meaning: "breath, wind, mind, seat of moral character and emotions" (Strong's Dictionary).

The Greek word for Spirit is - 'Pneuma' (Pronounced: newma) - meaning: "a current of air, breath, mental disposition; the power by which the human being feels, thinks and decides; the power that animates the body" (Strong's Dictionary).

Heart

Another important word to define is 'heart' because it is often used in reference to the immaterial part of man. The Hebrew word for heart is 'leb', and the *Greek word is –kapdia.* Strong's Dictionary defines heart as "the will and intellect; the centre of feelings; the inner man; the mind." Unger's Bible Dictionary defines it as, "the centre of the rational, spiritual nature of man; the centre of feelings and emotions; the centre of moral life, the centre of thought and conception; the centre of the entire man." As is shown, 'heart' is not in any way different from mind, spirit or soul; however, it is used mainly when referring to that which is in the centre or core of man's being; his disposition, motivations and the things which matter most to him. The Bible also shows that the heart can be in various conditions; for example, a pure heart, heavy heart, corrupt heart, evil heart, broken heart, joyful heart, a heart of grace and so on. We can postulate here that counsellors are essentially trying to mend the heart, or at least change its condition. This can only mean that counsellors, who acknowledge and understand the heart, are the more effective counsellors.

The Image of God

And God said, let us make man in our image, after our likeness... God created man in his own image, in the image of God created he him; male and female created he them. (Genesis 1:26-27).

Some scholars struggle with the fact that, the same Hebrew word 'Nephesh' (soul, living creature) is used to refer to both animals and humans, even though humans are far more sophisticated and intelligent. This is another factor that motivates some Christian scholars to distinguish between soul and spirit, therefore supporting the philosophy that man is made up of three parts; soul, spirit and body. Those who propose that man is made up of three parts, claim that the 'spirit' is the 'God-consciousness' in man and the element that separates him from animals. There is no need, however, for scholars to create their own theories to account for the obvious difference between humans and animals. The Bible speaks for itself, showing that man is made in the 'image of God' while all other creatures are made after their own kind (Genesis 1:25). Although both man and animals are called living creatures or living souls (Nephesh), the quality and ability of the soul of man are above that of the animal. After all, there are no religious or immoral animals anywhere, nor can there be. The point is that man is the offspring of God and is subsequently like Him, but animals are not.

The natural question now is, in what way is man like God? Firstly, the word 'image' which was translated from the Hebrew word *tselem* means "shade, resemblance"; "representative figure" (Strong's Dictionary). The word '*shade*' here is better understood as '*shadow*'; '*to cast a shadow*'. In clear terms, what the Bible is saying is that, man is a representation and a representative of God. Bible scholars conclude that the '*image of God*' is in reference to the qualities of God that have some counterpart in man. This means that the '*image of God*' refers to those qualities and abilities in God that man also has. Man is like God in that: God is a Spirit, so is man;

God creates complex things, so do men. The Godhead (Father, Son and Holy Spirit) fellowships, so do men. God's word has power to affect change, likewise men. God has dominion and is eternal, likewise men but not animals. Overall, man's attributes, abilities and qualities that he shares with God, is his likeness to God. His ability to know God, fellowship with Him and partake in His nature is what sets him apart from all animals. Note, however, that the image of God is something man is and not what he does.

A Unified Being

We have established that man is made of spirit (soul or mind) and body; however, counsellors must understand that man is a unity of material and immaterial substances that affect each other. He is two parts but one being. The brain is physical, but the mind/soul is immaterial. The point is, the mind is not the brain. Counsellors who believe that man is purely material and without 'spirit', are at a disadvantage in helping clients. One who does not acknowledge the immaterial part of man will only address the material part in problem-solving; such individuals are more medical doctors than counsellors. The fact is, the majority of counselling cases are concerned with issues in the immaterial part of man. Additionally, some of the problems (disease) in the material part (body) of man are as a result of psychological disturbances. The medical field has a term for this called 'psychosomatic disease'; *psycho = mind; somatic = body*. That is to say, an unhealthy mind will produce an unhealthy body. This very truth was first found in Scripture; a good example is Proverbs 3:5-8, which teaches that trusting, obeying and depending on God will bring healing and refreshment to the body. This confirms that there is a direct correlation between the material and the immaterial part of man; only death separates them. Proverbs 18:14 is another example which states that *"The spirit of a man will sustain his infirmity; but a wounded spirit who can bear?"* This shows that when the body is hurting, the mind/soul can help the person endure the pain, but when the mind or soul/spirit is broken, it is unbearable. This also indicates that psychological pain can be far worse than physical pain. This is something that all counsellors need to keep in mind as they seek to help those who are struggling and suffering. Here concludes the nature of man.

The Purpose, Role and Function of Man

Now that it is established that man is a unique creature made in God's image, we must now consider his purpose, role and function. Why was he made (purpose)? Where does he fit in the puzzle of creation (role)? And what is his duty (function)? A counsellor must have the correct answer to these questions if he intends to be effective.

The Purpose of Man

When we say 'purpose' what we mean is, 'why was man created?' In the words of the Creator Himself: *"... I have* ***created him for my glory****, I have formed him; yea, I have made him" (Isaiah 43:7). "Whether therefore ye eat, or drink, or whatsoever ye do,* ***do all to the glory of God****" (1Corinthians 10:31). "This people have I formed for myself; they shall* ***shew forth my praise****" (Isaiah 43:21). "Thou art worthy, O Lord, to receive glory and honour and power: for thou hast created all things, and* ***for thy pleasure*** *they are and were created" (Revelation 4:11). "Let your light so shine before men, that they may see your good works, and* ***glorify your Father*** *which is in heaven" (Matthew 5:16).* According to these passages, man was made for God's pleasure and glory; pleasure in the same sense that a newlywed couple decides to have children because it pleases them to have those bundles of joy running around their home. Glory, on the other hand, means the majesty, grandeur, greatness, honour, beauty, power and abundance that God possesses; to say the least. Man was created to carry, display and spread this glory of God. This means that the sum of all that man is and does should glorify God (Matthew 5:16). The purpose for man's existence then is strictly to satisfy God.

The Role of Man

Let us now consider man's role in the Universe. By role we mean the part he plays in the universe, his position and how he fits into the larger scheme of things. Let us consider these passages: *"For thou hast made him a* ***little lower than the angels****, and hast crowned him with glory and honour. Thou madest him to have dominion over the works of thy hands; thou hast put all things under his feet"* (Psalms 8:5). *"And God blessed them, and God said unto them, Be fruitful, and multiply, and replenish the earth, and subdue it: and* ***have dominion*** *over the fish of the sea, and over the fowl of the air, and* ***over every living thing*** *that moveth upon the earth"* (Genesis 1:28). *"Forasmuch then as we are the* ***offspring of God****..."* (Acts 17:29). *"Which was the son of Enos, which was the son of Seth, which was the son of Adam, which was the* ***son of God****"* (Luke 3:38). These few passages point out two important facts; firstly, that man is the son of God and secondly that he is the ruler/manager of the Earth. We could sum this up by saying that man is the son and representative of God, who is appointed chief and ruler of the earth, under the authority of God. Think about a good son who is responsible for his father's business.

The Function of Man

If man is the son of God and ruler of the Earth, created to glorify God, what are the tasks, duties and responsibilities given to him? How does he glorify God and fulfil his role as a ruler? Well, there are three main functions of man, and they are all about God: *Obedience*, *Fellowship,* and *Service.*

Obedience

"Behold, to obey is better than sacrifice..." (1 Samuel 15:22).

"And keep the charge of the LORD thy God, to walk in his ways, to keep his statutes, and his commandments, and his judgments, and his testimonies, as it is written in the law of Moses, that thou mayest prosper in all that thou doest, and whithersoever thou turnest thyself..." (1Kings 2:3).

"Now therefore, if ye will obey my voice indeed, and keep my covenant, then ye shall be a peculiar treasure unto me above all people: for all the earth is mine..." (Exodus 19:5).

"Let us hear the conclusion of the whole matter: Fear God, and keep his commandments: for this is the whole duty of man" (Ecclesiastes 12:13).

God has a plan for the universe and a plan for every person's life which cannot be accomplished without man's co-operation. Hence, the Bible is filled with commandments, instructions and guidance for man to live a godly and pleasant life. Man cannot accomplish anything worthwhile or fulfil his purpose in life without following God's directives. After all, man is completely dependent on God for breath, life, health, strength, prosperity and wisdom (John 15). It is in man's best interest then to cooperate with God. No father is pleased or glorified by his son's disobedience; hence, obedience is a prerequisite to glorifying God. Many people are having serious difficulties in life because they are constantly doing the opposite of what God requires; to which there are consequences. The wise counsellor will seek out the area of disobedience in his counselee's life, bearing in mind that some persons are completely ignorant to the fact that they are rebelling against God.

Service

"For we are his workmanship, created in Christ Jesus unto good works, which God hath before ordained that we should walk in them" (Ephesians 2:10). Man was created as a co-worker with God; therefore, God has assigned to him certain tasks that only he among earthly beings can do. Let us consider man's main responsibilities.

1. ***To care for the Earth***: *"And the Lord God took the man, and put him into the garden of Eden to dress it and to keep it"* (Genesis 2:15). *"So ye shall not pollute the land wherein ye*

are..." (Numbers 35:33). As ruler of the Earth, man is responsible for taking care of it by replenishing its resources and maintaining the proper order that is conducive to a healthy life. This means that man should refrain from any practice that pillages, pollutes and destroys the Earth.

2. ***To care for one another***: *"Pure religion and undefiled before God and the Father is this, To visit the fatherless and widows in their affliction, and to keep himself unspotted from the world"* (James 1:27). *"This is my commandment, That ye love one another, as I have loved you"* (John 15:12). "*We then that are strong ought to bear the infirmities of the weak, and not to please ourselves"* (Romans 15:1). *"Let each of you look not only to his own interests, but also to the interests of others"* (Philippians 2:4 ESV).

3. ***Replenish and reproduce***: "*And God blessed them, and God said unto them, Be fruitful, and multiply, and replenish the earth, and subdue it: and have dominion over the fish of the sea, and over the fowl of the air, and over every living thing that moveth upon the earth"* (Genesis 1:28). In the beginning, God made one man and one woman, since that time, it has been man's responsibility 'to make man'- through reproduction, thereby filling the Earth. This is a way of spreading the glory of God, since human beings are made in God's image. Notice that there were no limitations given; therefore, this idea that the Earth is overpopulated is ludicrous. As mentioned before, it is man's responsibility to properly cultivate, replenish and manage the resources of the Earth - to support its own population.

4. ***To spread the knowledge of God***: *"And he said unto them,* Go ye *into all the world, and preach the gospel to every creature"* (Mark 16:15). *"Declare his glory among the heathen, his wonders among all people"* (Psalms 93:3). *"Let*

the word of Christ dwell in you richly in all wisdom; teaching and admonishing one another in psalms and hymns and spiritual songs, singing with grace in your hearts to the Lord" (Colossians 3:16). Since man has the responsibility of glorifying God, it is necessary that he shares his knowledge and experience about God with others, to perpetuate the truth and the glorification of God.

5. ***Personal vocation**: "I therefore, the prisoner of the Lord, beseech you that ye walk worthy of the vocation wherewith ye are called" (Ephesians 4:1). "And he gave some, apostles; and some, prophets; and some, evangelists; and some, pastors and teachers; For the perfecting of the saints, for the work of the ministry, for the edifying of the body of Christ..." (Ephesians 4:11:12). "As every man hath received the gift, even so minister the same one to another, as good stewards of the manifold grace of God" (1 Peter 4:10).* All people are called into special assignments for God; counselling is one of them. All of us as individuals must find our unique God-given role and function and pursue it. We must seek to discover our unique gifts and abilities, in order to fulfil God's will and glorify Him.

Fellowship

"But the hour cometh, and now is, when the true worshippers shall worship the Father in spirit and in truth: for the Father seeketh such to worship him. God is a Spirit: and they that worship him must worship him in spirit and in truth" (John 4:23-24).

"Sing unto God, sing praises to his name: extol him that rideth upon the heavens by his name JAH, and rejoice before him" (Psalm 68:4).

By fellowship, we mean relationship, worship and communion. Man must have a relationship with God; after all, God is his father. Man must spend time seeking and communing with God through prayer, meditation, fasting, studying His Word, holy living and worshipping, through music and dance. *"Draw nigh to God, and he will draw nigh to you..."* says Apostle James, the biological brother of Jesus *(James 4:8). "Come now, and let us reason together, saith the LORD..." (Isaiah 1:18).* It is clear from these verses that God expects man to relate to Him in a mutual, loving relationship. He requires men to love, seek, trust and praise Him with their entire being. Worship and fellowship are a great part of the reason why man was given the ability to know and relate to God. As mention before, Jesus (God incarnate) told His disciples that they were His friends, "*Greater love hath no man than this that a man lay down his life for his friends. Ye are my friends, if ye do whatsoever I command you*" (John 15:12). God wants relationship, that's the bottom line. "*For thus saith the Lord unto the house of Israel, seek ye me, and ye shall live* (Amos 5:4)." *"Behold, I stand at the door and knock; if anyone hears My voice and opens the door, I will come in to him and will dine with him, and he with Me"* (Revelation 3:20). Worshipping Yahweh has positive effects on a person's being. When a person comes in contact with God, they are coming in contact with goodness, love, joy, hope and peace. Fellowshipping with God then, has the potential to restore, rejuvenate and energise the body and mind (Psalms 16).

As is shown, Man is a spiritual being with an earthly body. He is the son of God; the bearer of His glory. He is the master of the earth, the crown of creation, an earthly being with heavenly obligations. He is the object of God's love; God's representation.

CHAPTER 4

What is Man's Problem?

When one ponders on the weakness, frailty, delinquencies and immorality of man, one cannot help but ask, 'what's wrong with man?' Philosophers, theologians and religious leaders have been trying to answer this question for centuries. Clearly, man recognizes that there is something about himself that is not right. Murder, lying, stealing, insulting, cheating, selfishness, self-centredness, jealousy and diseases are just a few of the phenomena that make life unpleasant. Of course, there are those like the Hedonists, who do not subscribe to the idea that there is something wrong with man; rather, they excuse and embrace the delinquencies and immorality of man. This hedonistic philosophy reflects one of the great flaws of humanity, which is the tendency to embrace what is wrong and harmful for self and others. In any case, the Bible is clear that something is wrong with man; fortunately, it also provides a solution.

The Bible teaches that an angel called Satan, decided to rebel against God, thereby introducing '*Sin*' which corrupted God's perfect creation (Isaiah 14, Ezekiel 28, Romans 8:20, 1 John 3:8, John 8:44). This resulted in the onset of misery, pain and evil in the universe. Satan the father of sin and the adversary of God, later influenced the first man and woman (Adam and Eve) to also rebel against God, thereby corrupting their perfect nature; herein lies the beginning of man's problems (Genesis 3:1-24).

What is Sin?

There are several words in the Bible, both Hebrew and Greek, that are translated '*Sin*'. For the sake of brevity, only a few will be looked at here, and then a summary of the various words will be provided.

***Hebrew**: **Chattah** - an offence. **Pawsah** - to rebel. **Avon** - to pervert. **Asham** - to be guilty, to be at fault.*

***Greek**: **Harmatia** - to miss the mark. **Anomia** - lawlessness, iniquity. **Parabasis** - Transgress, go beyond boundaries.*

In short, sin is offending God, rebelling against Him, breaking His laws, perverting the good and failing to meet God's demands.

The Bible further categorises sin under three umbrellas: The *lust of the flesh*; *the lust of the eyes* and *the pride of life* (1 John 2:16). The lust of the flesh speaks of all inordinate desires and love for sensual pleasure; it is the overindulgence and the gratification of insatiable bodily appetites (food, sex, drugs, etc.). The lust of the eye speaks of the inordinate desire to have all that looks good, particularly material possession and wealth. The pride of life refers to the inordinate desire for status, glory, honour and fame. Now it is obvious that sensual pleasure, wealth and honour are not bad in themselves but the strong obsessive desire and the relentless pursuit of them, without regard for the command of God, is sin. Galatians 5:19 gives some insight into what sin looks like:

Now the works of the flesh are manifest, which are these; Adultery, fornication, uncleanness, lasciviousness. Idolatry, witchcraft, hatred, variance, emulations, wrath, strife, seditions, heresies. Envyings, murders, drunkenness, revellings, and such like of the which I tell you before, as I have also told you in time past, that they which do such things shall not inherit the kingdom of God.

Note that each of these items on the list is either offensive to God or harmful to human beings, whether it is the person doing it, or the one it is done to. Ultimately, sin destroys man, distorts his mind and separates him from the benefits of God.

The Nature of Sin and the Act of Sin

Galatians 5:19 is a list of sinful activities or behaviour which we call *acts of sin*, meaning these are sinful activities that a person chooses to do by his will. Behind these behaviours, however, the Bible teaches that there is a *nature of sin*, also called '*the flesh*'. This is the principle or law of sin that is at work in all people. It is this nature which causes people to commit sinful acts. This is the nature that Adam and Eve received from Satan after they rebelled against God. The Apostle Paul talks about this nature in Romans 5:12, and 7:18 respectively, "*Wherefore, as by one man sin entered into the world, and death by sin; and so death passed upon all men, for that all have sinned.*" "*For I know that in me (that is, in my flesh,) dwelleth no good thing: for to will is present with me; but how to perform that which is good I find not.*" Sin is hereditary; this is the issue that Paul is addressing here. The Bible shows that when Adam and Eve rebelled against God, they broke fellowship with Him. As a result, their wills were bent away from God, their minds became self-centred and their bodies also became subject to sickness and death. This became Adam's new nature which he passed on through his seed from generation to generation.

In Psalms 51:5, King David made reference to this nature inherited from Adam, stating, "*Behold, I was shapen in iniquity; and in sin did my mother conceive me*". Speaking on the same topic, he also stated elsewhere that, "*The wicked are estranged from the womb: they go astray as soon as they be born, speaking lies*" (Psalms 58:3). We must admit that even precious little babies are selfish, self-centred and disobedient, think about it. Why do we have to teach children the right things? And why is it so hard for them to learn it? They seem to learn the wrong things easily, even without a teacher. Let us face it, you never have to yell at a child, bribe them or punish them to learn the wrong things. It would seem as though the wrong things are easier to learn. The fact is, human nature is corrupt from birth. This knowledge about the sin nature seem to be common knowledge in the ancient world, for many of the prophets and writers from that time spoke of it, including the prophet Jeremiah who declared that, "*the heart is deceitful above all things, and desperately wicked: who can know it*?" (Jeremiah 17:9). The philosophy of the world today is that humans are innately good; on the contrary however, there is very little evidence of this in our art, entertainment, government, businesses and neighbourhoods.

We must agree with the Bible then that there is an evil, corrupt nature in man which propels him to commit acts of sin. Now let us be clear, God is not holding people responsible for their corrupt nature inherited from Adam; however, every person is responsible for his *acts of sin*, for it is with his will that he chooses to sin and to remain a sinner. God has made it possible for man to change that corrupt nature for a new nature, the very nature of God; man must choose and seek this nature. God demands that man choose His nature; failing to do so is sin and sin brings judgment. The Apostle Paul is a classic example of a man, who, after discovering his sin nature, turned to God for a new nature, and God delivered him. In Paul's own words; "*... the law of the Spirit of life in Christ Jesus hath made me free from* ***the law of sin and death***" (Romans 8:2). God will do the same for everyone that comes to him.

The Effects and Consequences of Sin

Physical Death: *"But of the tree of the knowledge of good and evil, thou shalt not eat of it: for in the day that thou eatest thereof thou shalt surely die" (Genesis 2:17). "Then shall the dust return to the earth as it was: and the spirit shall return unto God who gave it" (Ecclesiastes 12:7).* At 930 years old, Adam (the first man) died; had it not been for sin, believe it or not, Adam and Eve would still be alive today. We must understand that it was never God's intention for man to physically die; after all, man was made to be like God who is eternal. Unfortunately, because of sin, we all have to deal with the reality of death, for the ultimate result of sin is death (Romans 6:23).

Spiritual Death: *"And you hath he quickened, who were dead in trespasses and sins...Even when we were dead in sins, hath quickened us together with Christ, (by grace ye are saved;)" (Ephesians 2:1, 5).* Spiritual death refers to being out of fellowship with God; to be void of His Spirit and to lose intimate communion with Him. Since God is man's source of life and strength, to lose connection with Him is death. Man cannot be his full and true self without union with God. This also has implications on the mind, since God is man's true source of wisdom, truth and peace. These implications will be discussed later.

Sickness and Disease: *"Therefore also will I make thee sick in smiting thee, in making thee desolate because of thy sins" (Micah 6:13). "There is no soundness in my flesh because of your indignation there is no health in my bones because of my sin." (Psalms 38:3 ESV).* It goes without saying that if man is disconnected from God, naturally the effects on the body will be negative. This also brings us back to the term 'psychosomatic'; if the mind is troubled because of the guilt of sin, the body can also be negatively affected as a result. The point is, sickness is a by-product of sin.

Lack of peace; distress: *"But the wicked are like the troubled sea when it cannot rest, whose waters cast up mire and dirt. There is no peace, saith my God, to the wicked"* (Isaiah 57:20-21). *"Behold, O Lord; for I am in distress: my bowels are troubled; mine heart is turned within me; for I have grievously rebelled"* (Lamentations 1:20-21). Sin releases torment in the mind because God is man's source of peace, but sin breaks the connection with God.

Guilt, Shame and Disgrace: *"...O my God, I am ashamed and blush to lift up my face to thee, my God: for our iniquities are increased over our head, and our trespass is grown up unto the* *heavens" (Ezra 9:6). "Righteousness exalteth a nation: but sin is a reproach (disgrace) to any people" (Proverbs 14:34).* After Adam and Eve sinned and their eyes were open to see their nakedness, they hid from God because they were ashamed and guilty before God (Genesis 3:7, 10). It was mentioned in the previous section that the Hebrew word 'Asham' which is translated sin in the English Bible, means, 'to be guilty'. This shows a direct relation between sin and guilt; after all, sin is the breaking of the laws of God which makes one guilty. Guilt brings shame; it has the potential to severely impair a person's personality and behaviour if not dealt with appropriately. Guilt can cause a person to be at war with and within himself. This can lead to insecurity and self-esteem issues; depression, bi-polar and schizophrenic tendencies, among other internal disturbances.

Depression: King David sinned against God and his enemies tormented him, then he cried out to God from a sorrowful heart saying; *"My soul is also sore vexed: but thou, O Lord, how long? ... I am weary with my groaning; all the night make I my bed to swim; I water my couch with my tears. Mine eye is consumed because of grief..."* (Psalms 6:3, 6-7). There are several chapters of the Psalms dedicated to David's depression and grief. His problem was caused by his own sin and the stresses of life. However, David found comfort and healing when he communed with God. The prophet Elijah also had a moment of depression triggered by guilt and fear. He had sinned against God by failing to trust Him for protection, and by his unwillingness to die for the Lord. This deeply troubled him within, *"...and he requested for himself that he might die; and said, It is enough; now, O Lord, take away my life; for I am not better than my fathers"* (I Kings 19:4). Elijah was a mighty prophet who knew God; he should not have doubted His ability to protect him. It is this doubt that caused him to fear and flee. Failure to trust God is a sin, and this sin caused Elijah much grief and sorrow until he was reconciled with God. Not all forms of depression is caused by sin; however, it is important to note that abusing the body also counts as unrighteousness, which can trigger depressive states.

Desensitized Conscience: *"Having the understanding darkened, being alienated from the life of God through the ignorance that is in them, because of the blindness of their heart: Who being past feeling have given themselves over unto lasciviousness, to work all uncleanness with greediness" (Ephesians 4:18).* When people continue in sin, their conscience eventually gives way and is ultimately silenced; thereby allowing the person to continue to sin freely without guilt or remorse. This means that the person becomes more and more immoral without regard. In short, sin begets sin, and the abundance of sin kills the conscience, destroying the moral fabric in the person; ultimately, destroying their mind (Galatians 6:7). This is called reprobate mind which will be discussed in chapter five.

Slavery to Sin and Weak Will: *"Jesus answered them, Verily, verily, I say unto you, whosoever committeth sin is the servant of sin"* (John 8:34). Jesus tells us here that the one who lives a sinful life is a slave to the sin nature previously mentioned. This means that even when the person wants to stop the sinful behaviour, it may be next to impossible because it has control over them (slave). This is where addictions, obsessions and repetitive behaviours which are obviously unhealthy and unproductive come into play. Sinful habits therefore, weakens the willpower.

Hindered Prayers: *"But your iniquities have separated between you and your God, and your sins have hid his face from you, that he will not hear" (Isaiah 59:2). "Then my anger shall be kindled against them in that day, and I will forsake them, and I will hide my face from them..." (Deuteronomy 31:18).* Unless it is a prayer of repentance or a prayer for the display of the glory of God, those who continue to disobey, and disregard God have no guarantee their prayers will be answered. God is not obligated to those who continue to rebel against Him, his promises are for those who follow Jesus.

Shut out of the Kingdom: *"Now the works of the flesh are manifest, which are these; Adultery, fornication, uncleanness, lasciviousness, Idolatry, witchcraft, hatred, variance, emulations, wrath, strife, seditions, heresies, envyings, murders, drunkenness, revellings, and such like: of the which I tell you before, as I have also told you in time past, that they which do such things* ***shall not inherit the kingdom of God****"* (Galatians 5:19-20). The Bible defines the kingdom of God as righteousness, joy and peace in the Holy Spirit (Romans 14:17). Sinners will never experience these; not now, not ever, because these are gifts only for the followers of Jesus who are obedient sons of God. It is for them to experience and enjoy. It is true that those who follow God sometimes don't 'feel' these blessings; however, they are always available to them, and feelings have nothing to do with it.

Unholy Fear of God: The Bible teaches that man should fear God, meaning man should revere and honour Him. The righteous are in love with God; therefore, they are not scared of Him. Sinners, however, tend to develop a tormented type of fear. They are scared of God; fearful of His wrath; ignorant of His love. These people are constantly conscious of their sins and terrified of how God may respond. In some cases, it leads to paranoia (Genesis 3:10; Proverbs 28:1). Sometimes this fear develops into anger, hate and hostility towards God (Job 21:14-15, Psalm 83:2, John 3:20, 2 Peter 3:3-4). People who feel this way tend to have difficulties in other areas of life, particularly relationships.

Curses:*"But it shall come to pass, if thou wilt not hearken unto the voice of the LORD thy God, to observe to do all his commandments and his statutes which I command thee this day; that all these curses shall come upon thee and overtake thee"* (Deuteronomy 28:15, see also Genesis 3:18; 4:11). A curse is the opposite of blessings; in fact, the word literally means "to go down" or "to be condemned". Sin does just that, it brings you down or backwards in life. Sin then invokes curses the way righteousness invokes blessings.

Eternal Death: Unrepented and unforgiven sin causes man to be separated from fellowship and communion with God for eternity. The reality is that man's spirit will not be annihilated; he will not cease to exist after this present life but will move into a new state and dimension. Some people will go on to eternal life with God, some to eternal death which is absence from God's sweet presence forever. This is the spiritual death spoken of in Matthew 25:41, Romans 6:23, 2 Thessalonians 1:9 and Revelation 14:11; 20:11-15. Eternal death is eternal cut off from joy, peace and love. In other words, after physical death, all people (soul/spirit) will still exist; however, only the sons of God will have true life.

What we have covered so far is only some of the major consequences of sin; further study will reveal much more that will help the counsellor sharpen his discernment. Nevertheless, it is easy to see that sin is what is wrong with the world. Every human issue can be traced back to the breaking of some law of God. Counsellors who overlook this reality will never truly help their clients. Man was made to please God, whenever he fails in this, that failure begins to penetrate other areas of his life. Many people are going from counsellor to counsellor year after year with little results because counsellors fail to address the root of the issue, which is often sin. Some counsellors are more focused on being nice and non-offensive to their clients, but this should never be a focus. Solution and victory are the focus of counselling, and this sometimes requires uncomfortable confrontations. Sin is dangerous; in fact, deadly, therefore, it must be dealt with sternly and lovingly.

A Superior Anthropology

In the last two chapters, we learnt that man is the created son of God, made in God's image. He was created to rule the Earth and serve God in a loving relationship. Man is an eternal being made of flesh and spirit; far superior to animals. He has the ability to act, be and do what he desires; to reason, to know wrong from right and to love. Humans have a problem from which all their other problems derive, the Bible calls it Sin. The Bible also provides the remedy for Sin and shows that most of man's psychological, emotional and behavioural issues, reside in his spiritual part. In short, the Bible thoroughly discloses who and what man is; which is necessary knowledge for a counsellor. Biblical anthropology provides us with the purpose of man and the problem of man; this is particularly necessary if a counsellor intends to be effective in problem-solving. The *Diagnostic and Statistical Manual of Mental Disorders*, the bible of secular counsellors, has no such knowledge; however, the Biblical counsellor has the luxury of this knowledge which makes him effective and unique. Unfortunately, many secular counsellors build their practice on the man-made theories of counselling and psychology, and the amalgamation of various philosophies, with no full, proper and authoritative view of man; this approach cannot be effective.

CHAPTER 5
What is Mind?

Psychology is the study of behaviour and mental processes. Its goal is to explain, predict and influence behavioural and mental processes. Merriam-Webster's Dictionary sums it up as "the science of the mind and behaviour." Interestingly, the New Oxford American Dictionary shows that the word 'psychology' is derived from the Latin word '*psycholog*ia'. '*Psycho*' is derived from the Greek word '*psuche*' which as mentioned before means *breathe, spirit and soul. 'Logia' is* derived from the Greek word *'logos'* which means *'the word of', 'the study of' or 'doctrine'.* We conclude then that *psycho-logy* is *the study of the soul (spirit) or the doctrine of the soul.* Sigmund Freud who confirms this definition also operated under the same understanding of the word, he states:

> *Treatment of the psyche means therefore treatment of the soul. One could also understand it to mean treatment of sickness when it occurs in the life of the soul. This, however, is not the only meaning of these words. Treatment of the psyche means more than this. It means treatment arising from the soul, treatment of disturbances of the soul or body, with methods which first and immediately concern the soul of people* (Boyd, 2000, p. 4).

That being said, the next two chapters will explore psychology from a biblical perspective. The intent is by no means to show that the Bible teaches the modern psychology boasted in secular universities today. Of course, the psychology presented in the Scripture far predates modern psychology. Modern psychology is the amalgamation of the ideas of Greek philosophers as far back as Hippocrates, Socrates, Plato and Aristotle. In later years, their ideas were built upon to form the discipline called Psychology today. What began then as Greek philosophy has transformed into a so-called science. There are therefore two schools of psychology: The

Creator's revelation of the soul as presented in the Holy Scripture and the Greek philosophy of the soul, which is based on human introspection, speculation, theories and some observations. The Bible describes this as the wisdom of men versus the wisdom of God (I Corinthians 1). We are interested of course in the wisdom of God.

In chapter three it was shown that the words *soul, spirit, heart* and *mind* are used interchangeably throughout Scripture, therefore making it difficult to ascribe any exclusive or distinctive meaning to any of them. There are a few more Greek words that were not mentioned before but were also translated 'Mind' in the Bible. Adding these words will help to give us a more comprehensive understanding of the use of the word 'Mind' in the Bible.

Nous

"The seat of reflective consciousness, comprising the faculties of perception and understanding, and those of feeling, judging and determining; the faculty of knowing, the seat of understanding" (Vines Complete Expository Dictionary of Old and New Testament Words).

"The intellectual faculty, the understanding; reason in the narrower sense, as the capacity for spiritual truth, the higher powers of the soul; the faculty of perceiving divine things; of recognizing goodness and of hating evil" (Strong's Dictionary).

Dianoia

"A thinking through or over, a meditation, reflecting. The faculty of knowing, understanding or moral reflection" (Vine's Complete Expository Dictionary of Old and New Testament Words).

"The mind as a faculty of understanding, feeling, desiring" (Strong's Dictionary).

Ennoia

"An idea, notion. Intent" (Vine's).

Noema

"Thought, design" (Vine's).

These words can be summarized in this way: 'Mind' is the inner part of man where his thinking, feeling, perceiving, intending and understanding happens; it is also the place where information is stored. *The Dictionary of Judaism in the Biblical Period* defines it this way:

> *Soul is the innermost part, most vital and intimate part of a human being-the part that is sentient, decision making, morally responsible, subject to emotion and feelings, susceptible to religious experience, and liable to divine judgment. It is considered one's true self... In the Hebrew Bible the terms "soul" and "spirit" are similar in meaning when they denote an aspect of the human personality. In general, there is also no clear-cut distinction in biblical literature between a person's "soul" or "spirit" and "body": the person is a unified whole* (p. 599).

On that note, from this point on, we will refer to the soul, spirit, mind and heart under one comprehensive biblical term, "the Inner Man". This term is used in the Bible to refer to the immaterial part of man; it can be found in the following passages, among others: Proverbs 20:27, 2 Corinthians 4:16, Ephesians 3:16.

THE INNER MAN

Its Origin

Genesis 2:7 tells us that God breathed into the physical body of man and he became a living soul. The physical body of man is made from the soil. This body, however, was lifeless and unconscious until God breathed into it. Note that the Hebrew word (Nshamah) that was translated 'breath' in Genesis 2:7 is sometimes translated ‘spirit.’ The point here is that, God placed a spirit in man’s body and at that point man became a living being. It means then that every person has an *inner man* who originated from God; therefore, all souls belong to Him and return to Him (Ecclesiastes 12:7; Ezekiel 18:4). After all, He created everything in the universe (John 1:1).

Its Nature

It has been established that the inner man is ***immaterial***, meaning it is intangible and cannot be seen with the human eye. The inner man is also ***eternal.*** The Scriptures show that the righteous will go on to eternal life after this present world while the wicked, rebellious and unbelieving will go to eternal punishment (Daniel 12:2-3, Ecclesiastes 12:7 Matthew 25:46). This brings us to the next point; the inner man is ***punishable*** and will be punished if he is not conformed to the image of Christ. This punishment can be as extreme as the total destruction of the inner man (Matthew 25:46, Daniel 12:2, Revelation 20:10, 14-15). Meaning that, while the inner man will still exist after the body dies, he will be void of the goodness, joy, peace and the presence of God; this is eternal torment.

The inner man can also be ***pure or corrupt*** (Matthew 5:8, Genesis 6:5, 2 Chronicles 12:14). Biblically speaking, pure can be defined as thoughts, deeds, desires and motivations that honour God. A corrupt inner man on the other hand is one that is turned away from God and is preoccupied with self and sin (Philippians 4:8-9, Romans 1:25-31). As stated before, people are born with a corrupt inner man due to the corruption of the first human beings who then passed this corrupt nature to all of humanity (Psalms 51:5, Jeremiah 17:9, Romans 5:12). The danger of corruption in the inner man is that, after prolonged corruption, it is possible for the inner man to become ***reprobate***; meaning, the mind is rejected and disapproved by God. The reprobate inner man is powerless against sinful desires since God is the only force against sin and the reprobate inner man is void of God's presence and power. The end result is an inescapable and perpetually sinful mind and lifestyle (Romans 1:28). The conclusion here is that, when the inner man is not conformed to the will of Jesus Christ, His righteousness and truth, it ***malfunctions***; this results in various maladies of the soul (inner man). Such maladies include depression, anxiety, fear, worry, bitterness, wrath, double mind, pride, lust and self-centredness to name a few (Galatians 5:19-21, Proverbs 12:25, James 1:14-15, Psalms 42, 1 John 4:18, James 3:16). It is necessary to note here that biblical counselling aims to heal and purify the soul (Roman 10:10).

The inner man is also ***divisible***. This means that a person can have a ***double or split mind***; that is, he can hold two or more different dispositions at the same time (James 1:8, James 4:8, Mark 9:24). A common example would be folks who continue in a relationship they don't want to be in. You see, they want to be in a relationship, but not this particular one; therefore, day after day, they are in constant conflict with their partner, never having a peaceful relationship. These are the people who break up every three months and get back together after a month. The point is, there are two opposing or conflicting ideas held in mind at the same time. They want to be in the relationship and not be in the relationship at the same time. They desire and reject their partner at the same time. This double-mindedness is often the cause and/or effect of doubt, confusion, multiple personalities and other manifestations of neurosis. Interestingly, the word 'schizophrenia' is Greek, meaning, 'to split mind'; or two souls (*skhizein* - to split; *phren* - mind). Could it be that many who have been diagnosed with schizophrenia are struggling with deception, doubt, confusion and double lives, leading to the double-mindedness and split personalities which often characterise these patients? Bear in mind that the inner man is vulnerable to deception, including self-deception. We have heard of extreme cases of pathological liars who tell lies that even they themselves believe (1 John 1:8, James 1:22-26, Jeremiah 49:16). This type of unhealthy use of the mind will lead to psychological issues like those seen in schizophrenia patients. It is important for counsellors to understand that at the heart of many counselling cases, there is a lie that the counselee has believed; this will be further discussed later.

The inner man is also ***unknowable***; it cannot be fully known or understood by humans. Let's face it, we are learning about ourselves daily, no matter how old we are. We still occasionally get surprised by our own words and deeds because we simply do not know ourselves as well as we think. Not that we cannot know anything about the inner man, for certainly, the Scripture has revealed enough. However, it cannot be fully understood or explained by any man; hence, the multiple views and theories about the soul, spirit, mind and behaviour of man. Of course, the truth about man resides with the creator, only He fully knows the inner man (I Kings 8:39, Jeremiah 17:9). In truth, counselling is a divine work; subsequently, only God and the people He uses can truly counsel, heal and purify the soul; a purely human method will not suffice.

Finally, the inner man is also ***changeable*** and susceptible to influences. The inner man is affected by thoughts, words and experiences, whether from within itself or from outside influences (Mark 7:20-22, Proverbs 23:7, Hebrew 4:12, Proverbs 12:25, Psalm 119:11). The Bible teaches that the inner man can be broken. When people speak of a broken heart, a broken spirit or a wounded spirit, they are talking about a real experience that is happening in the inner man. It often manifests as depression, despair, grief, sorrow and discouragement on various levels (Psalm 147:3, Psalm 34:18, Proverbs 15:13, Proverbs 17:22). This means that the inner man can take on different states of being, such as, strong or weak, joyful or sad, wise or foolish (Psalm 49:3, Proverbs 23:15, Proverbs 10:8, Proverbs 17:22, Psalm 42:11). Note that, from a biblical perspective, to be wise means to revere God; God intern grants wisdom to such persons, giving them the ability to understand life and spiritual things (Psalms 111:10, Daniel 5:12). This is generally the case of a biblical counsellor. On the other hand, a fool, according to the Bible, is one who does not believe in God. One who has no regard for God or for the things of God; he is therefore void of the knowledge of God (Psalm 14). This says much about counsellors who do not rely on God. The important thing to learn here is that **the inner man is capable of being transformed, reformed and restored**, which the Bible promises to do for those who believe and follow its teachings, and Jesus, the Christ (Romans 12:2, Ephesians 4:22-24 Psalms 23:3). On the contrary, many secular counsellors have no hope that their client's condition will ever completely change. What they believe is that a little medication and perpetual counselling will be enough to help their clients cope with daily life, but no real transformation, healing or change is expected.

Its Purpose

By purpose, we mean 'why'; specifically, why was the inner man created? We have already dealt with the purpose of the whole man, which cannot be separated from the purpose of the inner man. The outer man needs the inner man, and the inner man needs the outer man to function and to fulfil purpose. It allows a person to interact with the world around him and the world within him; to commune with others in the natural world and with spirits in the immaterial realm. It is the inner man that has the capacity to be like God, and to relate to Him, which is central to man's existence and purpose (Matthew 5:48, Romans 8:29, 1 John 3:2). No man, however, can be like God without following the path of Jesus; He is the only one who ever fully revealed God. In short, as it is for the whole man, the inner man was created to glorify God but more specifically to help man relate to God.

Its Function

By function we mean, what does the inner man really do? What is the actual task that he performs? The first task is ***Information Processing*** (Proverbs 15:28, Matthew 15:19, Philippians 4:4-9): The inner man receives information, analyses it, meditates on it, and ponders over it or as we commonly say, think. The inner man is capable of receiving information from both the visible and invisible world (spiritual realm). Information from the spiritual realm comes through visions, dreams, intuition, revelations and actual contact with spiritual entities (Numbers 12:26, Joel 2:28, Matthew 16:13-17). Information processing also leads to the formation of beliefs, ideas, desires, new perspectives, new affections, decisions and behaviours (I Kings 10:7, Romans 10:10; 13:12, John 20:31). Thoughts are the raw material forming a person's attitude and personality; it is the driving force directing their life path (Genesis 6:5, Proverbs 4:23, Proverbs 23:7, Proverbs 12:25, Romans 12:2). It is true that environment and experiences help to shape a person's attitude and personality; however, what a person thinks will ultimately determine who they are and what they become. We can conclude based upon what is said so far about the information processing function of the inner man that it is the inner man who allows a person to communicate with other entities and to be self-aware. Information processing also includes the ability to remember; the Bible does not speak about memory as a task of the brain but of the heart (Proverbs 4:20-22, Jeremiah 17:1, Psalm 119:11). It is interesting to note that this truth is also found in Chinese culture. The word 'forget' in the Chinese language is represented by a symbol (pictorial word) that actually means, "*escape the heart*". This is not to suggest that, the brain has nothing to do with memory. It is the brain's job to relay to the outer world what is happening on the inside of the person. If the brain is damaged, however, this hinders the process of transferring information from the inner man to the outer world. Scientific research in Alzheimer's disease shows that the shrinking of the brain causes memory loss because the brain's recollection capacity is damaged. The problem here is not that the person has lost the information but that the brain fails to recall it; assuming the information was stored in the first place.

Seeing: The inner man also has the function of seeing (Hosea 14:9, Ephesians 4:18, John 12:40, Proverbs 16:21). We are not talking about eyesight; rather, we are talking about the ability to perceive, to understand, to imagine and to be wise. This also includes vision and dreams which were previously mentioned. What we are saying here is that the inner man enables the person to see, discover and understand his environment, himself, others, and the spiritual realm. This can be summed up as intelligence or wisdom, which is to see with the heart. People often find themselves in a bad situation because of poor choices they made, based upon a distorted view of reality. This phenomenon of not being able to see is called blindness of the heart, darkened mind and more commonly, ignorance.

Affections (Matthew 22:37, Mark 12:31, Luke 6:35, Romans 5:5, Romans 12:10, 1Timothy 1:5): It is normal to associate the heart with love, and rightfully so because the same concept is found in Scripture. Scripture teaches that men ought to love God with all their mind, heart and soul (the inner man). It also teaches that man is the object of God's love; therefore, he is necessarily designed to know and experience love (John 3:16, Romans 8: 37-39, 1 John 3:1). In short, the inner man was made to love and receive love; this is basic to the purpose of his existence. The Scripture is clear however, that, although love is generated from the inner man, the evidence of its existence is found in one's personal attitude and behaviour. In other words, love is action (1 Corinthians 13, 1 John 3:18). Love will be further discussed later.

Aversive emotions (Psalm 38:8, 18, Proverbs 12:25, Ecclesiastes 7:9, 1 Corinthians 5:8, and Ephesians 4:31, 2 Timothy 1:7, James 1:20, 1 John 4:18): A word should be said here about negative or aversive emotions, such as wrath, bitterness, anxiety, fear, grief, worry, depression etc. These phenomena were not originally intended to be a part of man's experience. It is true that they too are processed and generated by the inner man or in other terms, they too find their home in the heart and are a legitimate part of the human experience. They, however, should not be classified as a function of the inner man but rather a malfunction, misuse, compromise or distortion of the inner man. They are the result of the fallen, sinful nature of man which resulted in faulty (unrighteous, irrational) thinking and behaviour. The Bible classifies these aversive emotions as sin, or the result of sin. Sin can easily be defined here as failing to use the mind the way it is supposed to be used, and for the purpose it was intended for. It can also be defined as the violation of the principles of God, or failing to use the heart to love according to God's law of love; this results in negative thought patterns, unhealthy emotions and inappropriate behaviours (1 John 4:18). If no intervention is done, a destructive cycle of sin and aversive emotions are set in motion. The good news is that the Bible teaches how to overcome this toxicity of the inner man (John 16:33, Colossians 1:13-14).

The conscience (Romans 2:15, Titus 1:15, Hebrew 10:22, I Peter 3:16): The Greek word used in the Bible for 'conscience' is 'suneidesis' which literally means, "a knowing with" or "a co-knowledge (with oneself)." Vine's dictionary also offers the following explanation: 1) "that faculty by which we apprehend the will of God, as that which is designed to govern our lives; 2) the sense of guiltiness before God; 3) that process of thought which distinguishes what it considers morally good or bad, commending the good." In simple terms, the conscience is the seat of moral consciousness and it is found in the inner man. It governs the thoughts and behaviour of the whole person, indicating when he is morally wrong and when he is right. Romans 2:15 explains this well, it shows that the conscience bears witness of the person's conduct, making excuses for certain behaviours while accusing the person of others. The Scripture declares that "*Thou wilt keep him in perfect peace, whose mind is stayed on thee: because he trusteth in thee*" (Isaiah 26:3). This is to say that when the mind is being used the way it was intended to, which is to glorify God by standing in moral integrity; peace of mind is the result. On the other hand, verses like Proverbs 12:25, Luke 21:34 and Romans 8:6 show that when the mind is out of line with the will of God, negative feelings and mental torment floods in. Conscience indicates a person's good or bad standing with himself, God and others, through positive and negative emotions. Like a system of rewards and punishment, the conscience offers peace or sorrow. King David who was familiar with these experiences once cried, "*For mine iniquities are gone over mine head: as an heavy burden they are too heavy for me*" (Psalms 38:4). David suffered from the terror of his own guilty conscience.

Enemies of the Inner man

We will briefly explore what the Bible has to say about things which are harmful to the inner man. Although some of this has been covered to a certain degree, it is important that we dedicate a section discussing this in more details. Let us begin with the most obvious enemy.

Negative Thoughts: Negative thoughts are those contrary to the thoughts of God; they are anti-life, anti-reality, unhealthy and harmful to self and others. Proverbs 27:3 shows that a person is what he thinks. Mark 7:21 shows that evil thinking leads to evil acts. James 3:14-17 and 4:1-2 also show that war, fights, envy and all manners of evil behaviour first begin in the heart. These thoughts drive men away from the presence of God where there is peace and joy (Psalms 16:11, Isaiah 26:3). Thoughts of fear, self-condemnation, impurity and wickedness are discouraged in Scripture because they bring torment to the soul. Scripture rather, encourages pure and lovely thoughts; thoughts of God, His promises and truth. These thoughts are healthy, keeping the soul on the right path and in peace (Luke 6:45, Romans 8:6, Philippians 4:8-9).

Negative Words: Words are vehicles for thoughts, meaning we only use words for the sake of sharing thoughts. It is appropriate then that we include *negative words* in this section on negative thoughts. We established that words, in general, affect the inner man; naturally, negative words have harmful effects. Proverbs 18:21 declares, "*Death and life [are] in the power of the tongue: and they that love it shall eat the fruit thereof.*" Words are not just wind, they have effect; words make men happy or sad, brave or fearful, zealous or discouraged. It is often an exchange of words that change lives, counselling is a perfect example. Negative words can harm the inner man; kill his dreams, motivation and self-esteem. The apostle Paul who knew this truth, implored believers in his '*letter to the Ephesians*', not to allow evil communication to come from their mouths but to utter words that will bless the hearers (Ephesians 4:29). He knew that God made the whole world with words; in fact, these words are still holding the world together now (Genesis 1, Hebrews 1:3, Hebrews 4:12); therefore, he knew that words are powerful enough to affect the inner man. The Apostle Peter also knew this truth, so he taught the believers saying, "*For he that will love life, and see good days, let him refrain his tongue from evil, and his lips that they speak no guile*" (1 Peter 3:10). The wise King Solomon concluded the matter in these words, *"a fool's mouth is his destruction, and his lips are the snare of his soul."*

The lesson here is that, words are seeds that we plant with our mouth and reap in our lives (soul). Bad seeds yield a bad crop.

Bad Experiences: These can be defined as those events in life that run counter to a person's desires, beliefs, expectations and personality, causing pain and misery. These experiences damage the personal status quo of an individual, often resulting in losses, whether material or nonmaterial; this includes traumatic events which can foster 'mental health' issues. Man was not originally made to have such unpleasant experiences. This is why people never automatically or naturally respond to negative experiences in a positive way. Bad experiences challenge the inner man to the core, often leaving him feeling powerless, angry, confused and discouraged. These experiences can have long-lasting effects on the inner man. Research shows that many children who were abused or traumatised are negatively affected right into their adult life, often developing personality issues (Swenson & Saldana, 2007). In the Bible, several stories depict individuals dealing with bad experiences. One such story is found in the book of Ruth. Naomi, a Jewish woman, was married with two sons in a foreign land (Moab) when her husband died. Eventually, her two sons died leaving behind their wives. Famine came upon the land, and Naomi had nothing to offer, so one of her daughters in law left. This poor woman lost all the men in her life in a short time; she had nothing left but one daughter in law who would not leave her. In her sorrow and pain, she exclaimed, *"Call me not Naomi, call me Mara: for the Almighty hath dealt very bitterly with me. I went out full, and the LORD hath brought me home again empty: why then call ye me Naomi, seeing the LORD hath testified against me, and the Almighty hath afflicted me"* (Ruth 1:21). This woman was broken by her loss. The name Naomi means 'pleasantness'; however, her bad experience took all her pleasantness, making her bitter; which is the meaning of the name Mara.

Another example can be found in the book of Job. Job was a wealthy man of God and father of ten children. He owned much livestock and property, but one day he lost it all. In one day, all his children and servants were killed, while some of his livestock was stolen and some killed (Job 1). Although Job was a strong believer, living a righteous life before God, such experiences had broken his inner man. Realizing his broken state, he cried, "*Why died I not from the womb? Why did I not give up the ghost when I came out of the belly?*" (Job 3:11). "*My soul is weary of my life; I will leave my complaint upon myself; I will speak in the bitterness of my soul*" (Job 10:1). Of course, he does not sound like a righteous man of God here, but that is the point, bad experiences can dry up all joy, peace and rationality in the inner man, only contact with God can reverse this. It is also important to add that a person's own unwise, inappropriate or ***ungodly behaviour*** can further disturb the inner man, considering that the conscience will cast judgement. As shown in the section on conscience, a guilty conscience will cause torment and sorrow in the inner man. Now it should be noted that wise counsel and right behaviour helps to reduce bad experiences; nevertheless, there are still those experiences and situations in life beyond a person's control. In these cases, wise counsel will help a person to respond in a wise, healthy and productive way to unwanted experiences. The advantage of the biblical approach here is that it offers a loving, all-powerful Saviour who cares and has the power to change any situation. Let's face it, there are those situations in life where no therapy, argument or theory will suffice; at that point, only a saviour is sufficient.

Sleep Deprivation: From the beginning, rest was instituted by God. We know that it is important to God that man rest because he also rested, as an example to man; although he needs no rest (Genesis 2:2-4). He also made rest apart of the Jewish law (Exodus 20:8-11). Let us understand that the word 'Sabbath' means 'rest'. Rest is a gift from God, and it is necessary for man's overall well-being (Psalm

127:2, Proverbs 3:21-24). In fact, Jesus announces that He came to give rest to those who come to Him (Matthew 11:28-29). Often, He would encourage His disciples to rest, as He himself would do (Mark 6:31). Now it is true that the Bible talks about a spiritual and eternal rest that God offers those who chose to follow Him. The Bible shows, however, that physical rest is important. Although Scripture does not go into detail concerning the consequences of sleep deprivation, the fact that God places so much emphasis on rest makes it clear that it is necessary and good. Even researchers have documented the negative effects of sleep deprivation; Professor David P. Murray reports in his paper on 'the theology of sleep' the following effects of sleep deprivation:

Intellectual Consequences

Sleep flushes dangerous proteins from your brain, improving mental health. When you are sleep deprived, you get a "dirty brain." Sleep allows the brain to consolidate and store the day's memories. Being exhausted zaps your focus and can render you more forgetful. Chronic sleep deprivation in adolescents diminishes the brain's ability to learn new information.

Emotional Consequences

Sleep loss produces apathy, irritability, weepiness, impatience, anger, and flattened responses. Sleep loss can cause psychological damage because sleep regulates the brain's flow of epinephrine, dopamine, and serotonin, chemicals closely associated with mood and behaviour. People with insomnia are ten times more likely to develop depression and seventeen times more likely to have significant anxiety. The lack of sleep affects the teenage brain in similar ways to the adult brain, only more so, and can lead to emotional issues like depression and aggression (p. 321).

Words like depression, anxiety, irritability, anger and apathy are clear indicators that the inner man is troubled when sleep deprived. In reality, sleep deprivation is the reason why many people are sitting before a counsellor. Wise counsellors always enquire about the clients sleeping habits.

Spirit beings: This is the major area where secular counsellors fall short because they are totally ignorant of spiritual things. This is unfortunate because activities in the spiritual realm account for many counselling issues. Man is a spiritual being; the inner man is that spiritual part of man which is immaterial, yet conscious and susceptible to influence. We have already established that man can communicate with God, who is a Spirit (John 4:24). This ability, however, is not exclusive to God; just about any spiritual being can communicate with man. Satan, the adversary of humanity, is real, and he has an army of demons (fallen angels/evil spirits) who influence, deceive, manipulate, oppress, depress, afflict, torment and possess humans (Matthew 25:41, Luke 4:33, Acts 19:13-16, 2 Corinthians 4:4, 1Timothy 4:1). Yes, demonic interference in human affairs is real; I speak from first-hand experience. One particular story in Mark 5:1-20, shows that, after Jesus defeated and removed demons which had possessed a man, this man, having been insane, was now in his right mind. This demonstrates that many counselling cases, especially those termed "mental illness," are spiritual at the root. The point is, sometimes the problem a person is having is inflicted or induced by evil spirits, even though the manifestation is observed in the inner and outer man. Let it be known that only counsellors who are led by Jesus Christ can help those who are spiritually oppressed. He alone has total authority and power over all spirits. God has mandated and equipped his ministers (counsellors) to cast out demons (evil spirits), release people from spiritual bondage and deliver them from the powers of darkness. Indeed, there is hope in Jesus for the spiritually oppressed (Matthew 10:1, Luke 10:17-19).

A final word about the inner man

The mind is the person, the inner person; the immaterial conscious person who occupies and uses the body. It is the personal headquarters, control room and government of an individual. It is in and through the mind that the entire human experience is happening. King Solomon being knowledgeable of this truth, wrote in Proverbs 4:23, *"Keep thy heart with all diligence; for out of it are the issues of life*." In other words, "*Be careful how you think; your life is shaped by your thoughts"* (GNT). Simply put, we should guard our minds. The apostle Paul says a similar thing in Ephesians 6:17 stating "*And take the helmet of salvation, and the sword of the Spirit, which is the word of God*." The apostle is saying that we should guard our minds with the truth God provides. The truth that we are His masterpiece created after His image and likeness. The truth that God loves us so much, He sent the Saviour to rescue those who would believe, from eternal damnation, curses, sin, sickness and evil spirits. As far as God is concerned, we are beautiful and perfect when we are in Christ, and He is in us. We can overcome this world, in Christ. In truth, those who believe have already overcome this world. Paul then goes a bit further by saying, "*Let this mind be in you, which was also in Christ Jesus*" (Philippians 2:5). This is a profound and logical statement. If mind is person and Jesus Christ is the perfect person, it makes perfect sense to take on the mind of Christ if we desire personal wholeness and a better human experience. Furthermore, the mind is made to serve God, to glorify Him and do His will; any other usage or purpose causes distortion and malfunction of the mind. Since Jesus perfectly fulfilled the will of God, thereby totally pleasing Him, it can only be wise to imitate Jesus in the pursuit of soundness of mind and a healthy personality.

CHAPTER 6
What is Mental Illness?

There are many controversy and debate over the definition of 'mental illness.' One of the problems with the term is that it is quite broad, vague and misleading. It is used to cover various types of cognitive, emotional, behavioural, neurological, physiological and spiritual abnormalities. However, The American Psychiatric Association (APA) gives the following definition:

> *Mental illnesses are health conditions involving changes in thinking, emotion or behaviour (or a combination of these). Mental illnesses are associated with distress and/or problems functioning in social, work or family activities* (www.psychiatry.org).

On their website, they go on to say that "Mental illness is nothing to be ashamed of. It is a medical problem, just like heart disease or diabetes". The problem here is that, the APA is authoritatively saying that mental illness is a medical problem, meaning that, the cause of mental illnesses can be found in the body; this is not entirely true. Contrary to popular belief, many so-called psychiatric disorders such as depression, bipolar disorder, personality disorder and the like have not been proven to have a physiological root. The chief editor of '*Psychological Medicine*', Dr Kenneth Kendler (Psychiatrist) reports that no neurological, neurochemical or genetical explanation for psychiatric disorders has been found (Kendler, 2005). Elliot Valenstein (neuroscience professor) and David Burns (psychiatrist & researcher) also found the same thing. They both report from their separate researches that no convincing evidence has been discovered to show that 'psychiatric disorders' are the result of dopamine, serotonin and norepinephrine deficiencies (Valenstein, 1998; Lacasse & Gamory, 2003). The fact of the matter is that much of what is labelled "mental illness" or "mental disease" has nothing to do with a biological, neurological or physiological problem, as many biblical examples will show.

This is no news to pioneer biblical counsellor Jay Adams who is known for highlighting the fact that many of the people who are labelled 'mentally ill' are usually people with unsolved personal problems rather than a brain disease. He argues that "true illness is organic"; meaning, there is an actual illness in the body, in which case, the person should be treated by a medical doctor, rather than a counsellor. It is certainly unfair to label people as 'mentally ill' because they are struggling to cope with their reality. The same way we would not label a person sick because they cannot run 100 meters in 9 seconds. What we are saying is, folks who have a psychological or behavioural issue caused by complications in the body should be separated from folks who are just struggling with personal, emotional and spiritual issues that are not physiological. Pastoral Counsellor, Paul Tautges, suggests the term "brain malfunction" to refer to those neurological issues which may affect a person's cognition, behaviour and development (Tautges, 2013). This is an appropriate term because it is clear about what it is referring to, removing all vagaries and generalisation. The point is that, there is a need for a distinction in diagnostic terminology and clarification of the term "mental illness".

Changes in thinking, emotion or behaviour caused by physical problems (neurological, hormonal, physiological and biological) should be labelled and treated separately from cognitive, emotional, spiritual and behavioural issues that are not rooted in the body and have not been proven to be so. That being said, I propose that mental illnesses have two forms: **physiological impairment** and **psychological disturbances**. Physiological impairment simply means that the cause of the apparent psychological and behavioural issues can be found in the body (e.g brain damage, brain disease, hormonal irregularities). Psychological disturbance, on the other hand, is emotional, spiritual, behavioural and mental experiences that are considered abnormal, unhealthy and unpleasant, but not caused by the body. Most counselees and so-called "mental health" patients fall into this category because they are not brain damaged or have some other medical condition affecting their thinking, feeling and behaviour.

Psychological Disturbances

Psychological disturbances can be further broken down into three major subcategories: *mental abuse, emotional mismanagement* and *spiritual torment.*

Mental Abuse: is the misuse and abuse of the mind; trauma and the resulting behaviours is the most obvious form of abuse. Mental abuse, however, also includes idle thoughts, impure thoughts, vain imagination, believing lies and the general failure to use the mind in a healthy/productive way. This includes failing to work, failing to put the mind to creative use, feeding the mind with the wrong things and of course, drug abuse, which also overlaps with the physical aspect, since drugs do affect the body (brain).

Emotional Mismanagement: simply means that a person is not healthily managing their emotions, resulting in various abnormal and unhealthy thinking and behaviour. It also means harbouring unhealthy emotions in the heart, like anger, unforgiveness, bitterness, jealousy, envy, hate, sadness, fear etc. For example, 22-year-old Anni lost her mother in a car accident. When Anni heard the news, she went into a shock and then denial. Anni refused to believe that it was true, she refused to talk to anyone about it, and she got angry when anyone referred to her mother as dead. Anni was in so much denial that she didn't even go to the funeral. Anni's whole life went on pause; she lost interest in all the things she used to love doing, while she grew in anger and bitterness. Over the next few years, she isolated herself and turned to alcohol to help her cope. She then spiralled down into depression and suicidal ideation. Nothing is wrong with Anni's body or brain; she has simply failed to cope with her mother's death and failed to grief in a healthy way. Anni doesn't need a doctor or medicine; she needs loving support to help her grieve properly, so she can overcome her loss healthy. The point is, when unpleasant and negative emotions are not properly addressed, they fester and worsen, causing much psychological pain and strange behaviour.

Spiritual Torment: can be defined as negative changes in thinking, emotion, behaviour and experience caused by wrong spiritual/religious association and practices. This includes interaction, influence and afflictions from spiritual entities. Wrong spiritual practices like witchcraft, necromancy, sorcery, spell casting, black magic and all forms of divination, invokes evil spirits; this is obviously dangerous and harmful to human life. Bear in mind that disobeying Yahweh-Yeshua is also a wrong spiritual practice that has consequences. Understand also that simply having the wrong beliefs and worshipping the wrong thing has negative effects spiritually and otherwise. Note also, that there are evil spirits (demons) that operate in a particular family for generations, much like hereditary diseases. These demons are call *"generational demons" or "family strongholds"*. These evil spirits may be assigned to a particular gender or birth order in the family; for example, all the first-born males in a family for ten generations may have serious anger problem or die at a certain age. Through the power of Christ however, these can all be defeated.

As we can see, mental illness is better defined as negative changes in thinking, emotion and behaviour caused by physical impairment or psychological disturbances. Biblical counsellors are aware of this truth; hence, it is their practice to send clients for medical check-ups to rule out the possibility of counselling someone who has a physical impairment and needs a medical doctor.

"Mental Illness" in the Bible

The term "mental illness" is not found in the Bible; nevertheless, it has examples of people who were deemed insane. We want to examine them for a biblical perspective on mental health. Let us first consider some of the terminology used throughout the Scripture to refer to insanity:

Anoia *(Greek) - without understanding (Timothy 3:9)*

Paraphronia (*Greek*) *- contrary to mind (2 Peter 2:16)*

Shigga 'own *(Hebrew) - craziness (Deuteronomy 28:28)*

Lunaticus (Latin) *- lunatic, moon sick, moonstruck (Matthew 17:14-18). "Affected with severely disordered state of mind"* (Merriam - Webster's Dictionary). Lunatic is sometimes used to refer to epileptics, which will be discussed later.

The madness of King Saul (1 Samuel 15-31)

"For rebellion is as the sin of witchcraft, and stubbornness is as iniquity and idolatry. Because thou hast rejected the word of the LORD, he hath also rejected thee from being king" (1 Samuel 15:22). These are the words of God to King Saul after he disobeyed God's command. After that, *"the Spirit of the LORD departed from Saul, and an evil spirit from the LORD troubled him"* (1 Samuel 16:14). It is interesting to note that the Hebrew word translated 'evil' in this verse is "Rah" which is also translated "heavy", "sad", "grief", "misery" and "distress". Some Bible translations, like Young's Literal Translation, appropriately use the phrase "spirit of sadness". The word 'troubled' in the same sentence is translated from the Hebrew word "ba' ath" which also means "fall upon" "terrify" and "dismay". We could say then that a spirit of depression or sadness or grief fell upon Saul causing him fear, misery and dismay.

Chapters 15 right through to 31 shows Saul's change in behaviour; he became quite irrational (1 Samuel 18:7-9). Now, when the young boy David, in the famous story of David and Goliath, defeated the enemy of Israel, the people of Israel praised him. Saul became angry, jealous and paranoid that the boy would soon take over His Kingdom. There was no reason at the time for the King to think such; rather, he should have been celebrating the victory of Israel. David was a boy whom Saul professed to love, a boy that saved Israel in a crucial battle; a boy that was Saul's therapist. How could he be so bitter towards him without legitimate reasons?

The chapters (15-31) further show that Saul became erratic in his behaviour, prophesying one minute and then trying to kill his therapist (David) the next (1Samuel 18:10-11). Saul spent the rest of his life devising schemes to kill David, who loved him and served him with loyalty. David was a fellow defender of Israel, he was Saul's son in law, his therapist and his son's best friend; yet he sought to kill him. Saul became so arrogant, fearful, paranoid and disconnected from reality that he ordered the death of eighty-five priests, a major violation in the Jewish culture at the time; all because he thought the priests were working with David. Saul did not stop there; he further ordered the onslaught of the entire city of Nob (city of the priests) killing even the animals and babies. This is rather bizarre behaviour for a man that was once anointed and appointed king of Israel. His bizarre behaviour goes further to the point where he stripped naked before the prophet and prophesied, lying naked on the ground all day and night; again, this is strange behaviour for a King (1Samuel 19:223-24). In the end, Saul committed suicide (1 Samuel 31:3-4).

Although this is but a brief overview of the story, the study shows that Saul's disobedience caused him to lose God's favour and Spirit, which left him vulnerable to evil spirits. These spirits left him afflicted with sadness, depression, dismay, paranoia, irrationality, rage, jealousy, pride and fear. The result was irrational behaviour, murder and ultimately suicide. It is important to highlight that all these words here can be used to describe the condition of the heart or the inner man. Note that the cause of Saul's drama of derangement is the absence of the Spirit of God in his life; this was brought on by his failure to obey the Word and command of God. Saul was without understanding, contrary to reason and disordered in his mind; this is the definition of madness. However, no biological or neurological reason was given for his malady and behaviour. The Scripture is clear that the Spirit of God left him and that was the beginning of his sorrows. This is not to say that occurrences in the body, particularly the brain, cannot affect thinking and behaviour; however, there is no reason or evidence for such diagnosis in the case of Saul, despite the clear fact that he was insane.

It was mentioned before that David was Saul's therapist because, whenever Saul was in his state of distress, under the power of the evil spirit, David would play music on his harp for Saul. This music therapy would bring Saul much needed relief from the evil spirit because they were songs of worship.

> *And it came to pass, when the evil spirit from God was upon Saul, that David took a harp, and played with his hand: so Saul was refreshed, and was well, and the evil spirit departed from him* (1 Samuel 16:23).

Some scholars argue that Saul was suffering from epilepsy, holding to the modern medical view that epilepsy is due to issues in the brain and not any supernatural phenomenon. The problem with the modern view of epilepsy, however, is that folks are diagnosed with epilepsy after two or more seizures. This method of diagnosis is insufficient because both biblical examples and modern cases of epilepsy show it to be more than just seizures. There are various forms and causes for seizures, many of which are still unknown; in any case, not all seizures are epilepsy related. The *Epilepsy Society*, which is the leading organisation dedicated to epilepsy research and awareness in the United Kingdom, reported on their website that 20% of the patients that come to them were wrongly diagnosed with epilepsy. They also expressed that epilepsy is difficult to manage. We can only conclude that this is due to the many variables and lack of knowledge concerning epilepsy. *Epilepsy Ontario,* a Canadian organisation dedicated to raising awareness and improving epilepsy education, released this revealing statement on their website:

> *For many people with epilepsy, the cause of their seizures is unknown. It is hoped that research and new developments in diagnostic testing will provide more answers for people with epilepsy and their families* (Epilepsy Ontario, 2018).

Could it be that the Greeks and the entire ancient world knew something about the unknown in epilepsy or lunacy? It was the universal belief in the ancient world that epilepsy was caused by supernatural agency. In fact, the name "epilepsia", which is Greek for "falling upon", was given to the condition by the Greeks. The name alludes to the idea of a bad spirit 'falling upon' a person, like the case of Saul. We must acknowledge the view of the ancient world because up until now, research on the causes of epilepsy is still not comprehensive or conclusive; therefore, full disclosure and understanding about the phenomenon are still limited. Researchers seem to know more about seizures than they do epilepsy; however, not all seizures are epilepsy related, and there are still seizures that researchers have not been able to figure out the cause of. That being said, we must stick with the biblical account of Saul's story that an evil spirit fell on him.

The madness of King Nebuchadnezzar (Daniel 4)

> *The king spake, and said, is not this great Babylon, that I have built for the house of the kingdom by the might of my power, and for the honour of my majesty? While the word was in the king's mouth, there fell a voice from heaven, saying, O king Nebuchadnezzar, to thee it is spoken; The kingdom is departed from thee. And they shall drive thee from men, and thy dwelling shall be with the beasts of the field: they shall make thee to eat grass as oxen, and seven times shall pass over thee, until thou*

> *know that the most High ruleth in the kingdom of men, and giveth it to whomsoever he will. The same hour was the thing fulfiled upon Nebuchadnezzar: and he was driven from men, and did eat grass as oxen, and his body was wet with the dew of heaven, till his hairs were grown like eagles' feathers, and his nails like birds' claws* (Daniel 4:30-33).

Before we get too far into this story, it is necessary to point out that, like the story of king Saul, this is a true historical event and not a myth or old legend. Now, Nebuchadnezzar's pride, arrogance, self-exaltation and failure to give God the glory for his success caused him to lose God's favour (Daniel 4:30, 37). Once he lost God's favour, he was driven mad and went to live in the wilderness among the animals, where he ate grass for over three years. The prophet Daniel counselled King Nebuchadnezzar to get rid of his sins by turning to righteousness. He suggested that he begin to take care of the poor, to ease the judgment that had come upon him. This was wise counsel because sin was the cause of his trouble and he needed redemption before God (Daniel 4: 27). In the end, the king turned to God, and he was healed of insanity. In his own words:

> *...at the end of the days I Nebuchadnezzar lifted up mine eyes unto heaven, and mine understanding returned unto me, and I blessed the most High, and I praised and honoured him that liveth forever, whose dominion is an everlasting dominion, and his kingdom is from generation to generation...* At the same time my reason returned unto me (Daniel 4:34-36).

King Nebuchadnezzar lost his mind and his ability to reason, then, he fell out of touch with reality because of his sin; the sin of pride in particular. Unlike Saul, however, he found redemption through repentance and lived. When he repented and turned back to God, his rational mind and understanding was returned to him. Once again, there is no evidence of any "organic" reason for his insanity and bizarre behaviour. What we know is that his relation to God was out of sync with the demands of God.

Other Insane People in the Bible

The lunatic boy (Matthew 17:14-18):

> *... there came to him a certain man, kneeling down to him, and saying, Lord, have mercy on my son: for he is lunatick, and sore vexed: for ofttimes he falleth into the fire, and oft into the water... And Jesus rebuked the devil; and he departed out of him: and the child was cured from that very hour.*

His bizarre behaviour was due to spiritual influence and afflictions, which Jesus fixed by getting rid of the spirit and its power over the young man. Every biblical counsellor and Christian person can have this authority if they desire.

The violent self-mutilating man (Mark 5:1-14):

A man with an impure spirit came from the tombs to meet him; this man lived in the tombs, and no one could bind him anymore, not even with a chain. For he had often been chained hand and foot, but he tore the chains apart and broke the irons on his feet. No one was strong enough to subdue him. Night and day among the tombs and in the hills, he would cry out and cut himself with stones. ...Then Jesus asked him, *"What is your name?"*

"My name is Legion," he replied, *"for we are many."* And he begged Jesus again and again not to send them out of the area. A large herd of pigs was feeding on the nearby hillside. The demons begged Jesus, *"Send us among the pigs; allow us to go into them."* He gave them permission, and the impure spirits came out and went into the pigs. ...and the people went out to see what had happened. When they came to Jesus, they saw the man who had been possessed by the legion of demons, sitting there, dressed and in his right mind.

Note that this man was influenced and troubled by many spirits at the same time; however, when they were removed, the man returned to his right state of mind. This is the case with many people today; multiple spirits influence and torment them in a subtle way, to avoid detection and removal.

Balaam the unrighteous prophet (Numbers 22-24):

> *Having eyes full of adultery, and that cannot cease from sin; beguiling unstable souls: an heart they have exercised with covetous practices; cursed children: Which have forsaken the right way, and are gone astray, following the way of Balaam the son of Bosor, who loved the wages of unrighteousness; But was rebuked for his iniquity: the dumb ass speaking with man's voice forbad the madness of the prophet* (2 Peter 2:14-16).

The apostle Peter classified this prophet as mad because he loved unrighteousness, which means he was disobedient to God.

The Bible clearly shows that not all cases of irrational, bizarre or erratic thinking and behaviour are physiologically initiated. It also shows that the unrighteous heart condition of a person can lead to insane thinking and behaviour, whether the heart condition is one of anger, jealousy, fear, pride, hate etc. Additionally, these negative conditions of the inner man seem to work hand in hand with spiritual entities (evil spirits/demons) that thrive off them, are drawn by them, often even initiated by them, to produce spiritual torment. One thing that seems to be common among the biblical cases of insanity is disobedience, dishonour or disregard for God in some way or other. It can also be observed that, from a biblical standpoint, mental health and stability to a great degree, is dependent on one's relationship with God. According to the great prophet of Israel, Isaiah, this is the case; he states, "*Thou wilt keep him in perfect peace, whose mind is stayed on thee: because he trusteth in thee*" (Isaiah 26:3). King Solomon also shares that same sentiment, stating that, "*The fear of the LORD is the beginning of wisdom: and the knowledge of the holy is understanding*" (Proverbs 9:10). With that said, could it be that many counselees just need to be reconciled to God and His Word? Once again, this is not to say that there are no neurological or biological causes for some people's mentality and behaviour; however, those are cases for the medical doctor and not the counsellor. Physical illness or diseases cannot be counselled, this is not to say that counselling is of no effect in such cases, however, the counsellor is not the primary physician then.

A Superior Psychology

What is unique about this biblical psychology is that it reaches beyond the material aspect of man and into the immaterial aspect; something secular counsellors and psychologists often fails to acknowledge. It is interesting to note that throughout the ages, the majority of philosophers and psychologists are atheists and agnostics trying to understand man apart from his creator and his spiritual nature. Gross and Simmons (2009) show that 50% of University professors are atheist, 11% are agnostics and that psychiatrists are the least religious of medical professionals. Needless to say, without proper study these men dismiss the Bible, calling it fictional, mythological and inaccurate. The Bible, however, has this to say to them:

> *For the preaching of the cross is to them that perish foolishness; but unto us which are saved it is the power of God. For it is written, I will destroy the wisdom of the wise, and will bring to nothing the understanding of the prudent... Because the foolishness of God is wiser than men; and the weakness of God is stronger than men... That no flesh should glory in his presence. But of him are ye in Christ Jesus, who of God is made unto us wisdom, and righteousness, and sanctification, and redemption: That, according as it is written, He that glorieth, let him glory in the Lord* (1 Corinthians 1:18-19, 29-31).

Here it is declared that the Word of God, which appears to be foolishness to those who think they are wise, is actually the wisdom of God. The passage shows that the doctrines of the Bible, particularly the Gospel of Jesus Christ; is the power of God to those whose soul it is saving. It further declares that Jesus has become the wisdom, righteousness, sanctification and redemption of the believer; hence, He is their saviour; the saviour of their soul.

Wisdom is the ability to discern and understand. *Righteousness* is the correct way to think, feel and behave. *Sanctification* is the process of restoration, putting back into the proper state that which has been tainted. *Redemptio*n refers to the act of God purchasing back humanity from the hands of his evil slave master (Satan) who subjected him to corruption (Sin). Wisdom, righteousness, sanctification and redemption are the necessary ingredients for fixing or saving the inner man. Jesus is the creator, giver and personification of these ingredients. He is indeed the key to biblical psychology; therefore, the counsellor that hopes to fix the inner man had better be familiar with Him. He is perfect personality; the template of the biblical counsellor. In conclusion, the Bible shows itself to be relevant in dealing with cognitive, emotional, spiritual and behavioural issues. It shows the way to God, His wisdom and His peace; peace beyond human understanding, peace that guards the inner man (Philippians 4:7). Ultimately, it shows the way to wholeness.

Although what has been presented in these two chapters is merely a glance at Scripture, it shows that the Bible is informative on matters concerning the human mind and behaviour. It reveals the origin of the soul, the perfect state of the soul, the corrupt soul, the remedy for a corrupt soul and how to develop and maintain a good healthy soul, to say the least. This body of knowledge that is rightly classified "psychology" is an in-depth, authoritative and insightful study of the human soul. What it reveals about the mind of man forms a solid toolkit for the counsellor to be effective in solving cognitive, emotional, spiritual and behavioural problems that are non-medical in nature. The Scripture provides ample teaching about fear, worry/anxiety, depression/hopelessness, emptiness, confusion, mental torment, double mindedness, lust, evil thinking, bad behaviour, emotions; lack of self-control, insanity and spirits. This type of teaching makes a counsellor competent to solve soul issues.

***See appendix for other contents of the Bible**

PART THREE
The Perfect Way

Counselling is directional. Counselling is the art of influencing or simply helping someone to move from one position to another, whether that position is psychological, relational or situational, the hope is to move to a better place. The counsellor and patient subsequently have a goal, a destination and the desired outcome that they are hoping for. The Bible is also directional. Contrary to popular belief, it is not a random collection of old tales. It is intentional and goal oriented; it has a path that leads somewhere far better than any counselling theory. In the next few chapters, the synchronicity and compatibility between the goal of counselling and the destination of Scripture will be explored. We will see that what counselling hopes to accomplish, the Bible accomplishes through a preeminent sociological order mandated by God; it shows a superior way leading to the best possible outcome in any situation.

CHAPTER 7
What is Love?

"And thou shalt love the Lord thy God with all thy heart, and with all thy soul, and with all thy mind, and with all thy strength: this is the first commandment. And the second is like (it), namely this, Thou shalt love thy neighbour as thyself. There is none other commandment greater than these" (Mark 12:30-31).

Humans are social beings by design. From the beginning, God declared that it is not good for man to be alone, He then instituted the family by giving Adam, the first man who ever lived, a wife; later on, they had children. If the creator of man says it is not good for man to be alone, we can conclude that relationships are necessary and vital for life. This fact is evident as early as infancy. Family therapist Maria Boccia reports that "secure attachment in infancy lays the foundation for healthy development and provides children with the beginning tools they need to reach their developmental potential" (Boccia, 2011, p.22). Boccia also reports that our first relationships shape who we are, what we believe about ourselves and our expectations of others. Interestingly, the ten commands that God gave to the Israelites are all about relationships. Four of the commandments are about man's relationship with God; the other six are about human relationships (Exodus 20:1-17). In counselling, only a few issues are entirely separate from the context of relationships. Grief, anger, fear, love, loneliness, rejection, jealousy, depression, pride, guilt, shame, personality disorder and the likes, are mostly within the context of some form of relationship, whether with self, others or God. Since relationships are so important to human well-being, it is necessary to study the dynamics and protocols of relationships from a biblical perspective. In the next few chapters we will explore relationships; however, this cannot be done without first defining love, since it is the common theme in Biblical relationships.

Love Defined

Among others, there are three particular words, both Hebrew and Greek which translate to "love" in the English versions of the Bible. These three words paint a vivid picture of what love really is:

Hebrew - "Ahava" - love; also means to give

Greek - "Agape"- love; goodwill, to prefer, to wish well

Greek - "Philos"- friendly, wish well, an associate

From these words we can gather that love means *to give, to be kind towards, to favour, to prefer and to associate with all others in complete good will.* The Bible describes what this looks like in practical terms.

1. Love forgives (John 3:16, 1 Peter 4:8).
2. Love corrects, confronts and disciplines (Proverbs 3:12, Matthew 18:15, Hebrew 12:6).
3. Love puts others first (Romans 12:10, 1 Corinthians 13:4-5, Ephesians 4:2).
4. Love adds value to a person (Proverbs 3:3-4, I Corinthians 13:2-4).
5. Love destroys fear (2 Timothy 1:17, 1 John 4:18).
6. Love is goodness (Psalms 106:1; 119:68, I John 4:16).
7. Love is the theme of life (1Corinthians13:13; 16:4, 2 Thessalonians 3:5, 1John 4:12-17).
8. Love is the law of life (Matthew 22:36-40, John 13:34-35; 15:12, Romans 13:8-13).

In summary, ***love is goodness (God) residing in a person, which is also extended to others.*** It is meditative and affective, active and demonstrative; in other words, it is inwards (affective) and outwards (active).

God wants us to know and experience love; in fact, He created man for love sake, therefore, loving and experiencing love is vital to human life. This is why God demands that we love each other, demonstrating His kindness and goodness at all times. In Jesus' Kingdom, love is the law and the rule of all relationships (Luke 6:31); even with enemies (Matthew 22:36-40). Hence, the Scripture urges us to do the same good to others that we want for our self. This is the law of the Kingdom.

Relationship with Self

Before we talk about *self-love* and *identity,* there are three different ways in which the word 'Self' is used in Scripture. For the sake of clarity, we will distinguish each.

- ***Self (A)****: sinful nature* - old self, the flesh, the part of man that causes him to sin; full of ungodly passions and lust; it is corrupt and in opposition to God; self-willed, self-centred, selfishness, self-seeking, egotistic and the likes (Romans 7:5; 8:8, Galatians 5:19-21; 6:8, Ephesians 2:3).
- ***Self (B)****: the conscious personality* - the whole being, referred to as me or I, a personal unique individual (Psalms 139:14-16, Luke 6:31; 9:23, Philippians 4:13, James 1:22).
- ***Self (C)****: man's true identity* - the real Self, the quickened Spirit, the new man, the Spirit of Christ in man (2 Corinthians 3:18; 5:17, Galatians 2:20, Colossians 3:10, 1 John 3:2; 4:17)

Now that we have defined 'Self', the real issue now is, how do we relate to each '*Self*'? The Scripture teaches that:

- ***Self (A)*** – *the sinful nature*: must be denied, rejected, mortified, never trusted, controlled, transformed, transcended, purified; frankly put, it must die (Romans 12:1-2, Galatians 2:20; 5:24-25, Colossians 3:5, Ephesians 4:22-24, 2 Timothy 4:5, 1 Peter 2:11).

- ***Self (B)** – the whole person*: must be surrendered to God; committed to God and serve

  God (Psalm 100, Romans 6:13; 12:1-2, James 4:7).
- ***Self (C)** – the true self*: pursue it, imitate it, put it on, walk in it, abide in it, live for it, love it; be confident in it, die for it, be united with it and glory in it (Ezekiel 36:26, 2 Corinthians 5:17-18, Galatians 2:20, Colossians 1:27; 2:6-7, Ephesians 4:24, Philippians 1: 21, 1 John 3:2; 4:17).

Identity

Identity is important for counselling because upon identity other concepts such as self-love, self-image and self-worth are developed. Etymologically speaking, the word identity comes from the Latin word 'identitatem', which means 'sameness' or 'the same'. The way we use the word 'identical' makes this clearer, and so does the way we use the phrase, "I identify with that person." By this we mean, there is something about the person, their situation or experience that is the same as ours. The point here is that, when we speak of identity, we are really talking about the degree to which a person is like something or someone else. We can say that identity in some way is the measure of sameness. For example, we identify a person as being a part of a particular ethnic group simply because they look the same. The point is that, human identity is always in relation to and in the context of something else. This means, there is something that a person is like or trying to be like. Many people are struggling with identity issues because they have identified themselves with the wrong things and are trying to be like the wrong things. In general, people tend to create idols, whether tangible or imaginative, that they identify with and pursue. The problem here is that, man already has a unique God given identity, given to him for a purpose. Any other identity conflicts his being and hinders the possibility of him reaching his full potential. Man's true identity is in God (Genesis 1:26); since man was made in God's image, he is identified with God and should therefore emulate Him. Man is not God, but he ought to be like Him in character, morality and spirit. God is man's frame of reference (John 1:4, Act 17:28, 1 John 3:2, 1 Peter 1:16). If people intend to know who they truly are, so that they may materialise or actualise it, they must follow God (Deuteronomy 5:33, Psalm 119:133, Matthew 8:34). Jesus Christ is the true identity of man; He was fully human but totally united with God. All people can have that identity restored if they so desire. Imagine with me, that each person is a verse of Scripture. When a verse is taken out of its context in Scripture, it loses its meaning, value and power, only to become dangerous. This same is true for people who live outside the context of Yeshua, the creator of the unity (universe).

Self-centredness & Selfishness

Self-centredness is a common mistake people make in trying to get the most out of life. Self-centredness is the excessive preoccupation with one's sinful nature, personality and interest. What this means is that all the energy of the self-centred person is channelled into serving himself. Since man was created to serve God and others, self-centredness is harmful to human development and the social order (Galatians 6:3, Philippians 2:3). One cannot be self-centred, and God centred at the same time; therefore, self-centredness usurps the place of God in the heart. When God is replaced in the heart, identity is affected. We have established that identity requires two that are the same. Therefore, self cannot find identity in itself; identity must be found in another. Self-centeredness then is a form of self-deception, which lays the foundation for mental health issues. It goes without saying that self-deception and self-obsession are psychologically unhealthy.

Selfishness is the natural offspring of self-centredness. Where self-centredness is the preoccupation with self, selfishness is the lack of concern for the welfare and desires of others. It goes without saying, that if you are preoccupied with self, then you do not have time for the interest and welfare of others. Selfishness and self-centredness then, are two sides of the same coin. Selfish individuals struggle to give of themselves in any way to others; making sacrifices for others is not on their agenda. This means that selfish people cannot actually love. Love often requires putting the interested of others first, but the selfish are too self-centred to consider the needs of others. From here, self-seeking, self-dependence, self-exaltation, self-will, self-indulgence and the like are birth. The Scripture, however, condemns all of these because they deviate from God (love) and are harmful to man's soul and well-being (Isaiah 14).

Overall, man must be dependent on God the way a fetus needs its mother (Psalms 121:1-2, Proverbs 3:5-6; 16:9). Man must humble himself in the sight of God, which means that he is aware of who he is in relation to God, and accepts it (Ephesians 4:2, Philippians 2:3-8). Finally, man must seek the will of God because he was not created for himself, but for the purposes of God. This means that God-centredness or Christ-centeredness (knowing and following the will of God) is vital to a man's well-being and success in life (Ecclesiastes 12:13-14, Romans 12:1-2, 1 Peter 3:8-12).

Self-love

There is much debate over whether or not the Bible teaches self-love. This is partly due to some psychologists attempting to align the Scripture with their psychological theories. The arguments are primarily surrounding the phrase, "*love thy neighbour as thyself*", found severally in Scripture (Leviticus 19:18, Matthew 22:39). The interpretation that many psychologists who happen to be Christian give to this passage is that, learning to love self is necessary before one is able to love others. They go on to cite the lack of self-love as the root cause of other personality and social disorders. They teach that one must learn to love himself before he can build good self-esteem, healthy self-image and self-confidence; all of which they believe is necessary for forming good relationships with others. A careful study of Scripture, however, will show that what the Scripture refers to as "loving thyself" is nothing but the innate and instinctive desire to want what is good for yourself. It is a built-in mechanism that helps man avoid harm and seek survival. We cannot presuppose that animals love themselves; although it is observed that they will do anything to protect themselves and prolong their lives. God knows that man is wired for survival like any animal. He knows that innately, humans want the best for themselves, that they hate discomfort and wish no harm for themselves. A baby cries when he feels the pain of hunger, not because he loves himself but because he hates discomfort. On that note, God charges humanity saying that the same care and concern that each man has for himself, he should also have for everyone else. Makujina (1997) gives an excellent explanation of Exodus 19:18, stating:

> *Self-love does not refer to self-esteem as Christian psychologists claim... Biblical self-love is common to all, Christian and non-Christian, and in neither is it based on a conscious understanding of a person's value to God or the imago Dei. Further, self-love is instinctive, spontaneous, and effortless. It needs no lessons, encouragement, or therapy; impulse drives it, and consistency characterises it. In contrast to what psychologists hold, the respect and honour that it entails is not from self but from others* (p.224).

The point is that the self-love referred to in Scripture is not one that needs to be taught or developed, no more than a normal person has to be taught to jump out the way of a moving car. Note that although the Scripture alludes to the idea of self-love, it does not instruct, promote or demand it, possibly because it is natural and instinctive to seek your own well-being. In reality, People have difficulty loving each other; therefore, the Scripture instructs, promotes and demands love for one another. Psychologists who promote self-love should consider promoting self-acceptance instead. Self-acceptance is simply being satisfied with how and who God has made you.

Self-Worth

Pioneer biblical counsellor Jay Adams points out that self-worth is a by-product of being identified with God and not something to be pursued in and of itself (Adams, 1973). He also found that one who loves God and others will not have problems with self-concept; rather, he will humbly praise God for what He is doing within him. As stated before, contrary to secular psychological concepts, the Bible teaches that man should find his identity in Christ, Jesus. The true basis for self-worth then is to identify with God and accept His love (1 Corinthians 6:17; 12:27, Galatians 3:27-28, 1 Peter 2:9). When man comes to terms with who he is in Christ and the fact that God truly loves him, only then is he equipped to love others as himself, because the love of God within him constrains him to do so (John 1:12, Romans 5:5, 2 Corinthians 5:14, Colossians 3:1-3, 1 John 3:1-2).

In short, Scripture teaches us to love Christ who is the true Self; the higher self. This is the 'self' that man should cultivate, protect and invest in. 'Self A' on the other hand, should be denied, while God and others are put first (Colossians 2:1-8, 3:1, Ephesians 3:16). It is through identification with Christ and the reception of the love of God, that man truly lays a foundation for self-esteem, self-image, self-concept and self-worth. These are not found within man but in God; man can receive them when he subscribes to God. According to Wagner (1975):

Once we have this assurance of being somebody because we know we are loved unconditionally by the living God, we can dare to disregard the idea that we are nobody. We no longer need to deceive ourselves about our true self- identity: we know we are somebody to God (p.170).

Counsellors ought to be careful not to encourage broken, sinful humanity to build confidence in 'self', the same 'self' that is already failing them. It is simply dangerous and unhealthy to promote self-love and self-worth apart from the context of God and His Word. This tends to produce self-centredness, egotism, pride, high-mindedness, idolatry and narcissism. It is obvious that these sins are harmful to relationships and personal development. The fact is that, if man is apart from God, he cannot love even himself; neither does he have any worth. If a person desires to be in a healthy relationship with himself, he must first seek God, accept His love and love others. In doing so, his soul will be satisfied, lacking nothing (Psalms 64:4; 107:9, Matthew 6:33, Romans 8:28). To truly love one's self is to love Christ, the true Self; to truly love Christ is to love others. This is the law of God. The same also goes for believing in one's self. We should never believe in "Self A", in human 'flesh' for it shall surely fail; in fact, it cannot please God, and that is its failure (Romans 8:7) The proper way to believe in one's self is to believe in Jesus Christ, the true Self that lives within. He is the only Self that is worth loving and believing in; He never fails. He is perfect in all his ways.

CHAPTER 8
Loving God

In the beginning, man violated the terms of his perfect relationship with God; since that time, all relationships, in general, have been out of order, perverted and corrupt (Genesis 3). This perversion gave birth to hate, rage, murder, oppression and indifference among men. It is for these very reasons that Jesus Christ came; He came to liberate the poor, the oppressed, the lost, the condemned, the broken and those disenfranchised (Isaiah 61, Luke 4:18-19). In essence, Jesus' mission was to put man back into right relations with God. God is a king; in fact, He is the King of Kings (1Timothy 6:15, Revelation 17:14). He is the Most High; the Father of creation and the head of all beings (Deuteronomy 10:17, Genesis 14:19-20). He is the source of life and every good thing (John 6:57, James 1:57). The world and all that is in it belongs to Him (Psalms 24). He is holy and full of glory (Leviticus 11:44). He is the universal lawgiver, the God of mercy and grace; above all, He is love (Nehemiah 9:31, Romans 11:22, 1 John 4:16). Now, the million-dollar question is, how do we as mere humans relate to such a being, what constitutes a right relationship with Him? The King speaks for Himself:

1. *Thou shalt have no other gods before me. Thou shalt not make unto thee any graven image, or any likeness of anything that is in heaven above, or that is in the earth beneath, or that is in the water under the earth. Thou shalt not bow down thyself to them, nor serve them (Exodus 20:3-5).*

   According to Yahweh-Yeshua Himself, man should worship nothing and no one but Him; to do otherwise is a violation of the terms of His relationship with man. This type of violation invokes the wrath of God (Colossians 3:5-6). What many secular counsellors fail to realise is that many of their clients have replaced the one true God with false gods, which have failed them. False gods and idols can be just about anything; anything that man holds dearer than God, from material things to immaterial things. House, cars, career, demons, imaginary figures, love ones, drugs, nature, even self can be an idol; as is often the case with atheists, who become their own gods, whether consciously or unconsciously. The problem with idolatry is that man's very existence depends on the one true God who is the source of life; He, therefore, cannot be replaced (Acts 17:28). The very breath man breathes is from Him, and so are peace, joy, strength and wisdom. Yahweh declares that He will turn against idolaters and cut them off; as was the case of Saul and Nebuchadnezzar and sadly the case of many counselees (Exodus 20:5, Ezekiel 14:1-8). The ramifications of being cut off from the source of life, joy, peace, love, wisdom and strength is nothing short of insanity. The bottom line is that serving other gods will invoke the wrath and judgement of the true God. Although there is no telling how the wrath of God may manifest in an individual's life, history shows that mental unrest is sometimes the case.

2. *Thou shalt not take the name of the Lord thy God in vain; for the Lord will not hold him guiltless that taketh his name in vain (Exodus 20:7).*

Yahweh is high, holy, honourable, full of glory and worthy of all praise; therefore, His name (s) should be handled with reverence. His name should not be associated with that which is not of Him. It should not be used for cursing, lying, deceiving or manipulating. It should not be handled with hypocrisy or used frivolously. Those who profess the name of the Lord should mean it when they use it. They should use it reverently and only in relation to what is truly God's. So many people profess to be of God, but they have ulterior motives. Some use the name of

God to take advantage of others; some to make themselves look good; while others use the Lord's name for false oaths, curse words and mockery. Yahweh is clear that He will charge those who use His name wrongfully. This means that, at the very least, favour, peace, joy and blessings will be reduced if not totally removed (Deuteronomy 28). It could be that many people are under this punishment (curse) unknowingly?

3. *And thou shalt love the LORD thy God with all thine heart, and with all thy soul, and with all thy might" (Deuteronomy 6:5, Matthew 22:37).*

   Man is commanded in this verse to love God with all his being (inner and outer); certainly, we are not just referring to an abstract emotional reaction to God. What then does it look like, or, what does it really mean for man to love God? The following four acts are required:

   a. **Obeying God** (Deuteronomy 11:1, 1 Samuel 15:22, John 14:15, 2 John 1:16): If man truly loves God, then this love is seen through obedience to God's Word and commands. Isn't the world full of horror and sorrow because of the constant breaking of God's laws and the total disregard of His Word? Love one another, even your enemies; don't murder, don't steal, don't cheat, don't lie, says the Creator; yet, here we are, in a broken, crooked, wicked world. Certainly, the world would be a much better place if we all obeyed God. His plan for man is always good; therefore, to deviate from His way is always a recipe for disaster (Psalms 128:1, Jeremiah 29:19).

   b. **Seeking God** (Deuteronomy 4:29, Psalms 14:2, Proverbs 8:17): The one that truly loves God will pursue Him. He will seek God's counsel, His presence and His favour. All that God promises, he will seek; especially His salvation and guidance. Man seeks God through, prayer, fasting, studying the Bible, meditation and dedication to righteous living.

c. **Worshipping/Serving** (Joshua 22:5, 1 Chronicles 16:23-31, John 4:21-24, Romans 12:1-2, 11): To worship is to honour, adore, celebrate, revere and obey. It is for this reason man was created; therefore, everything about him should honour God. We praise our children, spouses, parents and celebrities, downright worshipping them in some cases because worshipping is innate. All people worship something; even the so-called atheist, who either worships himself, nature, science or some ideology. God made man to worship; however, worshipping the wrong thing, robs man of blessings and God of glory. The whole world testifies of God's greatness and glory, but man has the greatest testimony and responsibility to worship Him (Psalms 66; 148). Man should worship God not only through faith and obedience but through actual singing and dancing unto God. Yes indeed, the holy, powerful, all loving God, Creator and Redeemer should be celebrated.

d. **Loving People** (Leviticus 19:18, Mark 12:31, 1John 3:18, 1John 4:11-21): It may come as a surprise that failing to love others is an automatic failure to love God. In fact, the Bible says that those who claim to love God yet fail to love others are liars. This means they do not love God at all; after all, man is God's image or shadow so to speak. To hate people, therefore, is to hate the image of God. However, loving only those who love us does not satisfy this command; rather, this command is about loving all people, including our enemies, strangers and those who are hard to love. Again, love is not only seen in emotional response but in attitude, behaviour and service toward others. To truly love people means to seek the best for them and to desire for them all the good we desire for ourself. Evidently, if all people lived in pure love towards one another, the need for professional counsellors would greatly diminish.

Benefits of Loving God

When man is in right standing with God, there are a series of blessings promised to him (Deuteronomy 28). Since these promises and blessings are too much to exhaust here, a selected few will be shown for their relevance in counselling matters.

1. **God's Love** (John 14:23, Psalms 37:28, Zephaniah 3:17, Romans 8: 35-39): God, who is perfect love, especially loves the obedient, showing it through His many blessings. God's love is never ending, never condemning, always forgiving and ever comforting (1 John 4). It is a pure love that keeps no record of wrongdoing. It is a self-sacrificing, unselfish love (1 Corinthians 13:5 GNT); a love all people desire and need. The Scripture shows that man is a love being; subsequently, love is essential for man's well-being (1 Corinthians 13:2-3). The neglected child, the hurting wife and the violent teenager are often sitting before a counsellor because they feel unloved. Love therefore, is the antidote for so many counselling cases. Those who follow Yeshua will experience and know the love of God.

2. **Peace/Protection** (Isaiah 26:3&12, Isaiah 54:17, Psalms 91:7, Luke 10:19, John 14:27, John 16:33): Most often, peace, both internally and externally is the goal of counselling. The anxious, fearful, paranoid, schizophrenic and drug addict often lack peace. True lasting peace however, only comes from God; it is a gift from God to the righteous. There is nothing then that man can do to generate true, lasting peace; drug addicts can attest to this fact. God offers a peace that is beyond human comprehension. It is a peace that is beyond our usual human experience of peace.

3. **Joy/Strength** (Nehemiah 8:10, Isaiah 35:10, Proverbs 10:28, Romans 15:13, 1 Peter 1:8-9): The depressed, discouraged, empty and suicidal are in search for joy, but there is nothing that man can do to create joy. Joy is not a product of humanity, like happiness. Happiness is dependent on what is happening; on the contrary, joy

comes only from God. Like peace, it is a spiritual blessing; it produces inner strength which allows people to cope with the challenges of life. Joy then is essential to human well-being.

4. **Wisdom/Understanding** (Job 28:28, Psalms 51&111:10, Daniel 2:21, 1 Corinthians 12:8, Colossian 2:23): The Bible teaches that there is the wisdom of the world and the wisdom of God (1 Corinthians 3:19-21). Naturally, the wisdom of God is far superior to that of man. Thankfully, much of this wisdom is found in the Bible. The wisdom of God is pure and should not be confused with the cleverness and craftiness of men. Many counselling cases could have been avoided had the counselee possessed the wisdom of God. Likewise, many counsellors would be far more effective had they the wisdom of God. Unfortunately, men who are not in right relationship with God cannot receive His blessed gift of wisdom and understanding. The gifts and blessings of God are for His people; those that are in right relations with Him (Deuteronomy 28).

5. **Forgiveness/Grace** (Psalms 86:5, Psalms 103:12, John 3:16, Titus 2:14, Hebrew 9:4, 1 John 1:9): Many people are ignorant of God's forgiveness, unable to forgive themselves or refuse to forgive others; hence, guilt and shame are common issues dealt with in counselling. Guilt and shame can be crippling; they hinder their victims from performing effectively and pleasing to God. The important part of this is that forgiveness is the antidote for guilt, shame, anger and bitterness amongst other things. Also, forgiveness means God has enabled us to live a victorious life over evil and sin, that we may go and sin no more. Understand that only the forgiven are empowered for victorious living. In any case, this forgiveness is available for those willing to enter into a right relationship with God through faith.

6. **Power over evil spirits** (Matthew 10:1, Mark 16:17, Luke 10:19, Acts 8:4-7): We have established that often times there are spiritual entities behind much of the behaviours and

phenomena labelled “mental illness”. Those who are in right relationship with God have been given the authority over such spirits, to subdue, rebuke and banish them from their presence. This is the great advantage of the truly Christian counsellor, for only he can deal with spiritual problems and spiritual entities correctly. All true believers have this authority in the spiritual realm, to take charge over evil spirits and to destroy their works. This is a necessary ability for victorious living.

7. **Eternal life/assurance** (Isaiah 32:17, John 3:36, John 11:25-26, Romans 5:21, Acts 17:31, Hebrew 5:9, 1 John 5:11-12): Eternal life is the quality of life that God has. His life has no end, no sorrow, no sin, no weakness and no evil but full of grace and power. If all people had this type of life, there would be no need for professional counsellors. The gift of eternal life gives assurance to the one who is in right relationship with God; regardless of the challenges they face in life, the eternal life of God is within them, enabling them to overcome. This produces confidence and contentment (2 Corinthians 4:17). It is also assuring for the believer to know that after this present earthly experience, a better life is coming in which there will be no evil, no sickness, no sin and none of what the devil brings; rather, they will live forever in perfect peace and harmony with God and all others (1 Thessalonians 4:17).

In summary, man’s relationship with God, affects his other relationships, his ability to effectively deal with life’s troubles and his quality of life. Furthermore, it affects his perception of the world; therefore, it is imperative that men seek God, know Him and please Him. Man’s life and success depend on it. The counsellor who refuses to stand on the Word of God robs his client of true lasting victory. The good news is, the Bible is an adequate guide for developing a wholesome relationship with God.

The way of Prayer

While we are on the topic of loving God, it is only natural that we talk about prayer; otherwise, the book would be incomplete. Now, prayer is access to God, access to heaven, the spiritual realm, power and wisdom. Counsellors need access to all of these if they intend to be effective. If counsellors do not have something beyond themselves to help their clients, they are extremely limited. Prayer is also communion; intimacy with God. It is simply talking to God, consulting him and fellowshipping with Him. When we talk with God, we get closer to Him; into His presence (James 4: 7-8). In His presence, there is fullness of joy, peace, comfort, healing and love. Counselees are seeking these things, and the counsellor cannot provide them; however, he should be a facilitator of them. He should lead his clients into the presence of God where they can encounter and experience Him; sometimes that is all it takes to solve a person's problem.

Prayer is power; power to change hearts and situations; power to break curses and invoke blessings; power to command evil spirits to cease from their works, release their victims and flee. Demons do not respond to psychotherapy they respond to the authority of God which praying people have access to. The solution to most counselee's issue is love; therefore, counselling should be done in an atmosphere of love. When a client sees his counsellor pouring out his heart to God on his behalf, it has a powerful effect on him; the effect of love. True prayer is indeed an exercise in love and God always responds to love.

No real counselling and lasting change can take place unless God is involved. Simply put, if God doesn't fix it, it's not fixed at all. The Bible also teaches that some issues can only be dealt with effectively through prayer (Mark 9:29). It is necessary then that counselling begins, continues and ends with prayer. In simple terms, what counsellors and counselee need, God has, and prayer can access it (James 5:16).

CHAPTER 9
Loving Others

"This is my commandment, that ye love one another, as I have loved you" (John 15:120).

The Family

A biblical perspective on the family is important to the discussion about the competency of the Bible in counselling; after all, numerous counselling cases are family related. Now, the family is a spiritual entity; a divine institution designed by God (Genesis 1:26-28). Ideally, it consists of a husband and a wife training up their desirable children into mature adults. Note that singleness, single parenting and childlessness are the exceptions to God's design and rule; nevertheless, these are families, and they should be treated as such. We can say the family is the bedrock of society, since society is made of people and all people are products of a family. The family is the microcosm on which the larger society is built. It is the first school, government and religion. The place where human beings first encounter each other, communicate, develop relationships, identity, self-concept, self-esteem and ideas about the value of other people. The family often has the greatest influence on behaviour, attitude and social life because the foundation for personality is laid there. The quality of the society then, is dependent on the quality of personalities produced by families.

The Bible has an in-depth study on the family which covers its origin, purpose, structure and guiding principles; however, for the sake of brevity, we will look only at what the Bible teaches about the roles and functions of the different members of the nuclear family. We have established that love is the theme, goal and law of all relationships; therefore, what we are looking at here is the way in which love is expressed through the different roles and functions of the members. Since the Scripture shows that sometimes friends are even closer and more valuable than relatives (1 Samuel 18:1, Proverbs 17:17; 18:24), we will assume that, what pertains to the family also pertains to true friendship. Note, however, that the Bible is clear that it is not a good idea to make friends with unrighteous and wicked men; perhaps they cannot truly be good friends (Proverbs 12:26; 22:24-25, 1 Corinthians 15:33). Now let us look at the different roles within the family.

Husband &Wife Relationship

> ***Husband***: *"Husbands, love [your] wives, and be not bitter against them" (Colossians 3:19).*
>
> *"So ought men to love their wives as their own bodies. He that loveth his wife loveth himself" (Ephesians 5:28).*
>
> *"Likewise, ye husbands, dwell with [them] according to knowledge, giving honour unto the wife, as unto the weaker vessel, and as being heirs together of the grace of life; that your prayers be not hindered"* (1 Peter 3:7).

The Scripture charges husbands to love their wives as their own body. In fact, it teaches that a husband and wife are one flesh; therefore, the rule to love thy neighbour as thyself is exemplified here more than anywhere else. Husbands must take their example from Jesus Christ, the husband of the church (Ephesians 5:25-28). Jesus sacrificed himself for the victory and well-being of the church. Likewise, God demands that husbands must gently care for, comfort, protect, provide for and lead their wives, without harshness and bitterness but with the love of God (Colossians 3:19, 1 Timothy 5:8). A man must nourish and cherish his wife, make her happy and enjoy her; not withholding his love and his body, which belongs to her (Deuteronomy 24:5, Proverbs 5:18-19, 1 Corinthians 7:3-5). The Scripture gives no lawful reason that will exempt a man from loving his wife; even if he puts her away in divorce, which the Scripture strongly discourages and only makes room for in the case of adultery (Matthew 10:2-12). In any case, even if a man divorces his wife, he is still expected to treat her with good will and well wishes (Romans 12:18, Ephesians 4:32). Finally, the Scripture rebukes adultery and divorce, demanding that men cherish their wives all the days of their life (Proverbs 5:15-18, Ecclesiastes 9:9).

> ***Wife*** *(Proverbs 31): "A virtuous woman is a crown to her husband: but she that maketh ashamed is as rottenness in his bones"* (Proverbs 12:4).
>
> *"Who can find a virtuous woman? For her price is far above rubies. The heart of her husband doth safely trust in her, so that he shall have no need of spoil. She will do him good and not evil all the days of her life"* (Proverbs 31:10-12).
>
> *"Nevertheless let every one of you in particular so love his wife even as himself; and the wife see that she reverence her husband"* (Ephesians 5:33).
>
> *"The aged women likewise, that they be in behaviour as becometh holiness, not false accusers, not given to much wine, teachers of good things; That they may teach the young women to be sober, to love their husbands, to love their children, To be discreet, chaste, keepers at home, good, obedient to their own husbands, that the word of God be not blasphemed"* (Titus 2:4).

These are only a few of the Scriptures about a wife's purpose, duty and place, in relation to her husband and the home. The Scripture is clear from the beginning that the woman was made for the man; to be his helper and equal partner in fulfilling the will of God on Earth. Together they are called one flesh, which means that they are two halves that need each other for maximum performance and productivity in life (Genesis 1:26-30; 2:18-25, Ecclesiastes 4:9). A wife is there to support her husband, a 'quarterback' of sorts; an assistant, there to watch his back. She is expected to respect him and submit to his love and authority, even in times of disagreement (Proverbs 21:9, Romans 12:21, 1 Peter 3:1-5). She must attend to her husband's need, not out of obligation but as an act of worship and obedience to God; never withholding her body and never giving herself to another (Exodus 20:14,1Corinthians 7:3-5, Colossians 3:18). She must take care of their home and children, and be an example of godliness (Proverbs 14:1, 1 Timothy 5:14, 1 Peter 3:1-5). God is the one who sets the standard for a wife. The Bible calls her, *"a gift from God"*, *"the favour of God"*, *"the crown of her husband"* and *"a good thing";* this is what God intends for her to be in relation to her husband (Proverbs 12:4; 18:22; 19:14).

Marriage

The Scripture shows that marriage is a holy partnership. It is a divine institution designed by God for one man and one woman to love, respect and honour each other unconditionally; serving each other and sharing everything for the length of their life. It is the God ordained institution and atmosphere for rearing children, character development, spiritual growth and training in love (Genesis 2:24). In short, marriage is meant to be enjoyed, but only when love is the anchor can it truly be enjoyed.

A word to the marriage counsellor: as is shown, marriage is God's institution; therefore, marriage must be in the context of God and His Word. After all, marriage vows are done onto God. Counsellors then must challenge couples to meet God's demand. At the root of every failing marriage is the failure to love in the way God demands. Couples are generally disgruntled because their needs are not met. This is usually due to selfishness and self-centredness at work in the marriage. Since love is the antidote for a failing marriage, every successful marriage must be built on God, who gives the ability to love even when it is hard. Some records show that finances are the number one reason why marriages fall apart. This only indicates that, instead of love, finances may be the number one reason for getting married. On that note, counsellors must remember to seek out the motive for marriage when dealing with couples; do not be surprised, however, that it may not be love. Finally, counsellors must remember that love is a behaviour and not just emotions. Love must be seen and not just felt. This visible practical love is what counsellors should demand. Note however, there is a difference between love and obsession. Obsession is a form of idolatry, which displeases God.

Parents and Children

Father: The biblical model of a father is God himself; hence, many of the Scriptures used to describe an earthly father's role and function, are Scriptures about God, who is the ultimate example. The Hebrew word for 'father' used in the Bible is '*AV*' which also means "*strength of the home*". The Bible further shows that the father is the leader of the home. He is also the priest, prophet, provider, protector, teacher/trainer and role model. He is God's representative to that home.

The father as ***leader, priest and prophet*** (1 Chronicles 9:13; 29:19, Proverbs 17:6, 1 Corinthians 11:3-16, Ephesians 5:22-24, 1 Peter 3:7): The biblical concept of leadership always entails serving others as opposed to being chief over others; this means that the main servant or the leading servant in the home is the father (Matthew 20:25-28, 1 Peter 5:3). ***As leader,*** he is the primary role model and final human authority in the home. ***As priest***, he represents his family before God. He prays for them, seeking God's mercy, will and favour for them (1Timothy 3:4). ***As prophet***, he represents God to his family. He teaches them the word, way and will of God (Deuteronomy 6:6-7). He is also the ***provider and protector*** of his family (Psalms 91:1, Proverbs 13:10, Matthew 7:11, John 15:13, 1 Timothy 5:8, 1 Peter 3:7). It is his responsibility to provide those things that are vital to life and well-being. Additional to that, he is responsible for his family's safety and security in every sense, from financial to physical and emotional security. ***As teacher/ trainer*** (Deuteronomy 6:6-9; 8:8, Psalms 78:5, Proverbs 4:1; 19:18; 22:6, 18), He is expected to teach his children the ways of God, the wisdom of God and the path of righteousness. He must teach them how to get along in society; to be productive, excellent and upright people. Since discipline is necessary for survival and success in life, it is a father's duty to teach and instil it. Foolishness is in a child's heart and the way to remove it is by disciplining that child, even as the heavenly father disciplines His children (Deuteronomy 8:5, Proverbs 13:24; 22:15, Hebrews 12:9). This should never be confused with abuse; the Bible shows that godly discipline is love (Hebrew 12:6). Finally, the Bible commands fathers not to provoke their children, or to stir up wrath in them, but to have compassion on them, less they become discouraged or broken in spirit (Colossian 3:2, Ephesians 6:4, Psalms 103:13). This, however, is no contradiction of terms; the Bible is clear that children should be disciplined, but this must be done in a loving, compassionate way.

A father's hard labour and sacrifice for the financial, emotional, spiritual, psychological and social well-being of his children is the expression of love; his love and the love of God. This labour of love is not optional, it is a father's God ordained duty. A father sacrifices his time, energy, resources, dreams and pleasures to invest in the well-being and success of his children in society. Above all, he labours to present them holy before his heavenly Father.

As a father models the heavenly Father before his children, teaching them the ways of God with loving compassion and mercy, his expressed love becomes a tower of strength for his children; releasing in them a sense of safety, security, confidence and peace. These are vital to a child's healthy upbringing. Research shows that loving relationships are beneficial and becomes a part of a person's psyche permanently. That is to say, a loving relationship with parents produces inner security and healthy self-concepts. Young offenders in the prison system testify of this fact; the majority of young men that enter the prison system have dysfunctional relationships with their father, or no father at all in their life. Some of these boys are ordered by the court to see counsellors and psychologists because of their behaviour. It is likely that these young men are emotionally, psychologically and socially tainted because they have been robbed of the love of a father; hence, their dysfunctional life of crime and anti-social behaviours. Fortunately, the counsellor who is skilled in using the Bible knows how to bring healing and comfort to the fatherless. They also know how to reconcile fathers with their children and how to train fathers to be excellent, through the use of Scripture (Malachi 4:6).

Mother: The Hebrew word for mother (eym) means "strong water"; water is a symbol of life, and indeed a mother is a life-giver, not just in birth but after birth she continues to give life to her home (Proverbs 31). Interestingly, the Hebrew people made glue by boiling animal skins in water. As the skin broke down, a thick sticky liquid formed at the surface of the water. This thick liquid was removed and used as a binding agent (glue), hence the term "strong water". The idea is that the mother is not only the life giver but the glue of the home; the one who binds the family together in love. She is an equal partner in parenting with the father; she is there to support, compliment and supplement him (Genesis 2:18-24). She too has the task of teaching and training her children; however, she has a greater responsibility in nurturing the child which begins in the womb (1 Samuel 1:23, Isaiah 66:13, Proverbs 1:8; 31:26-27). She like the father is a role model (2 Timothy 1:5, I Peter 3:4). She is expected to model godly character. Her obedience and respect for her husband is an example that teaches her children to obey and respect authority. Her quiet, gentle and kind spirit, which God requires of a woman, becomes a template for her children's personality. Mothers are homemakers; which means that, while the father is the leader in the home, the mother is often the manager of the home (Proverb 14:1, Proverbs 31:26-27, 1 Timothy 5:14, Titus 2:2-4). Fathers may supply raw materials, like a house, groceries, money and babies but a mother will yield a final product; such as, a happy, healthy, family home, where great men and women are nurtured and prepared physically and spiritually, to serve society.

According to one research done by Ohio University, children who grow up in married couple homes (two parent household) have a better environment for cognitive stimulation and emotional support (Grabmeier, 2009). This means that a mother and father working together in a home is the ideal setting for rearing emotionally intelligent children. Where fathers may be a symbol of God's authority, justice and security; mothers may be a symbol of God's compassion, mercy and peace. Father's tough love and mother's soft love, balances the child's view of God and his perception of the world. That being said, the Scripture demands an atmosphere of love in the home; complete love for God and one another. Of course, love for God is shown only in obedience to God and in service to one another.

In summary, parenting is a godly assignment; therefore, parents should not relate to their children according to their own feelings or according to the wisdom of men but according to the wisdom and love of God.

Children: *"Children, obey your parents in the Lord: for this is right. Honour thy father and mother; which is the first commandment with promise; that it may be well with thee, and thou mayest live long on the earth"* (Ephesians 6:4).

"Children, obey your parents in all things: for this is well pleasing unto the Lord" (Colossians 3:20).

Over and over again, the Scripture charges children to obey their parents; to honour them, to bless them and to take care of them; otherwise, their life experience will not be a pleasant one. This is a constant theme throughout the Bible (Exodus 20:12, Deuteronomy 21:18-20, Proverb 1:8-9; 30:17, Mark 7:10, 1Timothy 5:4). The Bible teaches that a child must follow his parent's instructions; otherwise, he who was meant to be a blessed joy to his parents becomes a burden and sorrow (Deuteronomy 12:16, Proverbs 17:25). Children ought to yield to their parent's discipline, never cursing but ever loving their parents through it all. In general, most children will submit to loving and godly authority and discipline; those who fail to do so, the Scripture refers to them as fools worthy of reprimanding or punishment (Proverbs 12:1; 13:24; 15:20 22:6). The Bible does not negate the fact that some children are difficult, disobedient, rebellious, foolish and wicked. In the days of Moses, adult children who behaved like this would be worthy of death; however, the Scripture shows that God has issued a new way and a new law through Jesus Christ. Because neither parents nor children are perfect in this present world, God has given a perfect way that will work perfectly for imperfect people; this is the way of love.

Love is patient and kind regardless of circumstances; love is always obedient to God. Many parents will have to seek their children's forgiveness and at the same time forgive their children; likewise, many children regardless of age may have to seek their parent's forgiveness and at the same time forgive their parents. The difficulties that families face are endless and sometimes uncontrollable but love covers sins, and it keeps no record of things done wrong. This is the basis for the biblical parent-child relationship (1 Corinthians 13:5, 1 Peter 4:8).

A final note should be made here about cultures that believe it is the children's responsibility to financially support their parents. While it is commendable that children look after their parents, the Bible demands that parents leave an inheritance for their children; even their grandchildren. That way each generation is better off than the one before, oppose to each generation maintaining the status quo. The point is that, parents should be doing their best to have something to give to their children rather than taking from them (Proverbs 13:22; 19:14).

The depth of Scripture on the subject of "family" goes far deeper than what has been presented here. The student of counselling must spend the time to study the Scripture in depth for its truth that transforms. The Bible has a solid doctrine on family relations that can help the counsellor to understand family dynamics, root problems and the rules of engagement in the home. Without any such authoritative body of knowledge about the family, it is impossible for a counsellor to be effective in problem-solving and counselling for families. Overall, the Bible makes it easy to counsel families because it has clear guidelines, rules and definitions. This makes it easy for the counsellor to figure out the area in which the family is out of sync with the sociological order of God.

Other Relationships

Employer: *"Thou shalt not oppress an hired servant that is poor and needy, whether he be of thy brethren, or of thy strangers that are in thy land within thy gates"* (Deuteronomy 24:14).

"Masters, give unto [your] servants that which is just and equal; knowing that ye also have a Master in heaven" (Colossians 4:1).

"Woe unto him that buildeth his house by unrighteousness, and his chambers by wrong; that useth his neighbour's service without wages, and giveth him not for his work;" (Jeremiah 22:13).

Employees: *"And whatsoever ye do, do [it] heartily, as to the Lord, and not unto men"* (Colossians 3:23).

"Servants, [be] subject to [your] masters with all fear; not only to the good and gentle, but also to the forward" (1 Peter 2:18-20).

"Servants, obey in all things [your] masters according to the flesh; not with eye service, as men pleasers; but in singleness of heart, fearing God" (Colossians 3:22).

The Bible rebukes both employer and employee for dishonesty and any ungodly conduct. It commands employers to be fair to their employees, not cheating them but giving them what is due. At the same time, it calls for employees to give of themselves to their employers as if unto God, not cheating them or giving them a hard time, even if they are difficult employers. We can see that the employer/ employee relationship is still subject to the law of love, goodwill, well-wishing and giving. This biblical work ethic is a good foundation for a counsellor to stand on when addressing disgruntled employees and abusive employers. Perhaps if this method was applied in all employment relationships, there would be less violence in workplaces and greater productivity in business endeavours.

***Strangers**: "Also thou shalt not oppress a stranger: for ye know the heart of a stranger, seeing ye were strangers in the land of Egypt"* (Exodus 23:9).

"Do not neglect to show hospitality to strangers, for by this some have entertained angels without knowing it" (Hebrew 13:2).

"For I was hungry, and you gave me something to eat; I was thirsty, and you gave me something to drink; I was a stranger, and you invited me in" (Matthew 25:35).

"Beloved, you are acting faithfully in whatever you accomplish for the brethren, and especially when they are strangers" (3 John 1:5).

In short, do onto strangers as you would have them do unto you, for you are a stranger as well. Again, the Scripture demands goodwill to all men, including the ones we don't know.

***Enemies**: "But I say unto you which hear, love your enemies, do good to them which hate you..." (Luke 6:27-28).*

"Dearly beloved, avenge not yourselves, but [rather] give place unto wrath: for it is written, Vengeance [is] mine; I will repay, saith the Lord. Therefore if thine enemy hunger, feed him; if he thirst, give him drink: for in so doing thou shalt heap coals of fire on his head" (Romans 12:20-21).

"Rejoice not when thine enemy falleth, and let not thine heart be glad when he stumbleth" (Proverbs 24:17).

Enemies can be a real opposition and threat to one's well-being; nevertheless, God requires that man leave wrath, judgment and revenge to Him. Man must continue to love, even those who are hard to love and those who refuse to return love.

***Government**: "Let every soul be subject unto the higher powers. For there is no power but of God: the powers that be are ordained of God. Whosoever therefore resisteth the power, resisteth the ordinance of God: and they that resist shall receive to themselves damnation"* (Romans 13:1-3).

"Render therefore to all their dues: tribute to whom tribute is due; custom to whom custom; fear to whom fear; honour to whom honour" (Romans 13:7).

"I exhort therefore, that, first of all, supplications, prayers, intercessions, and giving of thanks, be made for all men; For kings, and for all that are in authority; that we may lead a quiet and peaceable life in all godliness and honesty" (1Timothy 2:1-2).

The Scripture shows that all governmental authority is appointed of God, whether it may appear so or not. The Bible then calls for us to submit to their rule and to pray for them, which in itself is an act of love. The fact that God ordained the government however, does not automatically mean that they always obey God. When leadership contradicts the values, commands and doctrines of God, we should seek to please God before men, as is shown severally throughout Scripture (Proverbs 16:7, Daniel 3&6, Acts 5:29, Galatians 1:10).

A final word on Relationships

The Bible shows that human relationships are God's idea. It was created for the glory of God and for the benefit of man. It is an exercise in and of love for love sake. The theme, goal and law of relationships are authoritatively laid out in Scripture. It calls for love, goodwill, well wishes and favour for all men at all times under all circumstances. Additionally, the Bible shows that there is authority and hierarchy in the universe; subsequently, there is authority and hierarchy on Earth, even in relationships; after all, God is a God of order. God the Father is the head of all creation and the head of Christ; Christ is the head of the Church and the head of man, man is the head of woman and parents are the head of their children. Employers are the head of their workers and the government is the head of the nation. All authority must be respected, honoured, obeyed and loved; however, God must be honoured above all. Those in authority should never abuse or cheat those under their authority. People ought to serve one another, seek each other's best interest, forgive one another and keep the peace; in doing this, men show their honour, love and obedience to God. Certainly, the Bible presents a superior sociological order, which if truly applied by all people on Earth, would create a paradise. It is the job of the counsellor to hold men accountable to the sociological order of God. By doing so, he becomes a worthy gardener in God's paradise and a conduit of joy, peace and love. Now in the words of the Apostle Paul:

> *Love is patient and kind; it is not jealous or conceited or proud; love is not ill-mannered or selfish or irritable; love does not keep a record of wrongs; love is not happy with evil but is happy with the truth. Love never gives up; and its faith, hope, and patience never fail. Love is eternal* (I Corinthians 13:4-8 GNT).

CHAPTER 10

The Perfect Destination

If the Bible is relevant to counselling, there must be some compatibility or synchronicity between the goal of counselling and the goal of Scripture. To test this idea, we must first consider an official definition for counselling so that we may understand what it entails. The American Psychological Association gives the following definition on their website (2018):

> *Counseling psychology addresses the emotional, social, work, school and physical health concerns people may have at different stages in their lives, focusing on typical life stresses and more severe issues with which people may struggle as individuals and as a part of families, groups and organization. Counseling psychologists help people with physical, emotional and mental health issues improve their sense of well-being, alleviate feelings of distress and resolve crises. They also provide assessment, diagnosis, and treatment of more severe psychological symptoms (Counseling Psychology, 2018).*

The British Association of Counselling and Psychotherapy may have been the first association to define professional counselling back in 1986. Here is what they said:

> *Counselling is the skilled and principled use of relationship to facilitate self- knowledge, emotional acceptance and growth and the optimal development of personal resources. The overall aim is to provide an opportunity to work towards living more satisfyingly and resourcefully. Counselling relationships will vary according to need but may be concerned with developmental issues, addressing and resolving specific problems, making decisions, coping with crisis, developing personal insights and knowledge, working through feelings of inner conflict or improving relationships with others.*

These two organisations are international authorities in professional counselling; we can therefore assume that their definition and explanation of counselling is well developed. Based on their definitions we can summarise that, ***the goal of counselling is to solve human problems for the sake of enhancing well-being.*** According to the Oxford Dictionary, well-being means, "*The state of being comfortable, healthy, or happy.*" Oxford Thesaurus also renders the following words as synonyms for well-being: *welfare, good health, happiness, comfort, security, protection, prosperity, good, success, good fortune, advantage and successfulness.*

If counsellors are aiming to improve a person's well-being, it means that in some way the counsellor is a warrior combating the forces that threaten human welfare. These forces can be divided into four major categories, representing the root cause of common issues addressed in counselling. Keep in mind that we are discussing counselling primarily for psychological, spiritual, emotional, relational and behavioural issues. These major root causes are ***Death/Loss, Lies/ Ignorance, Lust/Inordinate Affection*** and ***Fear*** (see fig. 1).

Death/Loss: many people are sitting before a counsellor because of someone or something important in their life that has come to an end; they have experienced a loss and have failed to respond to this new reality healthily. An example would be the loss of meaning and purpose in life, perhaps the result of another loss, such as the loss of a loved one. A common manifestation, in this case, may be depression or confusion which can lead to an array of other issues like anger and mood swings. The obvious antidote for ***death/loss*** is **restoration**, **recovery** and **abundant life** which the counsellor will help the client to achieve.

Lies/Ignorance: many people are deceived, whether by self or others; in any case, they continue to believe and act upon lies which naturally have a negative effect on their lives. The same goes for ignorance, many people's difficulty in life is simply due to a lack of right knowledge (Hosea 4:6). An example would be a promiscuous young lady who is starving herself to achieve a certain physique; all because she believes that her self-worth is dependent on how attractive she is. Such a young lady needs to learn the truth that she is made in the image of God, that she is God's masterpiece; therefore, her value and worth is in God and cannot be measured. On that note, there is no need for her to destroy the temple of God (her body) to feel valuable or to be accepted. The natural antidote for ***lies and ignorance*** *then, is* ***knowledge of the truth***.

Lust/Inordinate affection: inordinate means excessive and unreasonable. Many counselees have been taken over by a disproportionate and irrational desire/love (obsession) for something, which in turn results in inappropriate behaviours and unhealthy lifestyles. An example would be a rich workaholic father who continues to neglect his family because of his insatiable appetite for money and power. The antidote for ***lust and inordinate affection*** is ***pure love*** with **self-control**. This workaholic father then needs to learn to convert his love for money and power into love for God and his family. He also needs to develop the ability to control his desire for money and power.

Fear: many people's behaviours are secretly driven by some fear. A good example would be a college student who keeps changing his area of study every two years, with the excuse that he has found a new interest, when in truth he is reacting to his fear of failure. His thinking (consciously or not) is that, as long as he never has to complete a program, he never has to face the possibility of failing. The antidote for ***fear*** is ***love*** *and* ***truth***, which produces assurance, confidence and courage (1 John 4:18).

We can agree that all these antidotes are prerequisites to being comfortable, healthy, happy, prosperous and secure. Now that we have a better understanding of what counsellors are battling in therapy, we can now revise the goal of counselling in light of these major root causes and their antidotes. The goal of counselling then, is to ***1) equip the counselee with truth*** that will ***2) enable him to give and receive pure love, 3) overcome fear, lies and ignorance, 4) restore what is lost, help him accept what cannot be restored*** and ***5) improve the quality of his life.***

The table does not show or label the various manifestations of psychological, spiritual, relational and behavioural problem; rather, it shows what lies behind or at the base of those manifestations (root causes).

Major Root Causes of Common Counselee Issues (fig. 1)

Death/Loss of	**Lies/Ignorance** About	**Inordinate Affection/** **Lust for**	**Fear** of
• Person • Relationship • Health • Love, Peace, Joy • Dreams/ambitions • Career/job • Purpose/meaning • Inner strength/willpower • Self-worth • Abilities/skill • Opportunities • Valuables/finances • Status/power/Control	• Self • God • Others • Life/world • Situations • Future • *Lies believed* • *Lies acted upon*	• Material things • Money • people (e.g. someone else's spouse) • Self • Earthly glory/praise • High Status/power • Pleasure • Pain	• Man • God (not reverence but terrified) • Spirits • Death/loss • Pain • Misfortune • Failure • Success • Change • Powerlessness • Losing Control

The Path of Scripture

Now that we have established the goal of counselling, we must now explore the goal of Scripture to finally test its synchronisation with the goal of counselling. However, before we can understand the destination of scripture, it is worthwhile to understand first, the path of Scripture.

"*All Scripture is given by inspiration of God, and is profitable for doctrine, for reproof, for correction, for instruction in righteousness...*" (2 Timothy 3:16). This verse leaves no doubt about the purpose of the Bible; it is given by God for instruction in righteousness. According to Unger's Bible Dictionary, *righteousness* means "purity of heart and rectitude of life; the being and doing right." Before the 16th century, '*righteousness*' was spelt '*right-wiseness'* which is a little more self-explanatory. In short, righteousness is thinking, feeling and doing right, in the sight of God.

King David of Israel made the following comment about the Scripture:

> *The law of the LORD is perfect, converting the soul: the testimony of the LORD is sure, making wise the simple. The statutes of the LORD are right, rejoicing the heart: the commandment of the LORD is pure, enlightening the eyes. The fear of the LORD is clean, enduring forever: the judgments of the LORD are true and righteous altogether. More to be desired are they than gold, yea, than much fine gold: sweeter also than honey and the honeycomb. Moreover by them is thy servant warned: and in keeping of them there is great reward. Who can understand his errors? Cleanse thou me from secret faults. Keep back thy servant also from presumptuous sins; let them not have dominion over me: then shall I be upright, and I shall be innocent from the great transgression. Let the words of my mouth, and the meditation of*

my heart, be acceptable in thy sight, O LORD, my strength, and my redeemer (Psalms 19:7-14).

King David makes it clear that the Word of God is intended to lead man into righteousness; however, he goes a little further to show that the Word of God also: **1)** converts the soul **2)** makes wise the simple **3)** rejoices the heart and **4)** warns about sin and pending troubles/judgment. In Psalms 1:1-2, David also declared that the benefits of righteousness are prosperity, productivity and vitality. Proverbs 12:21; 14:32 also confirms that it shall be well with those who follow righteousness but there will be sorrow for those who do not.

Another important passage of Scripture to share here is John 17:17, a prayer by Jesus Christ: "*Sanctify them through thy truth: thy word is truth.*" Here we learn two things: first, God wants to sanctify man, which simply means that God wants to make man like he ought to be in the first place. He wants to restore man, to cleanse him from all that taints him, to make him holy and perfect again (Ezekiel 36:26, 2 Corinthians 5:7, 2 Thessalonians 5:23). The word 'sanctification' also suggests a process; a process of change, not an instant or overnight change. Secondly, the verse also points out that the Word of God is the truth, and with truth, God will counsel, comfort and transform man, that he may have a more pleasant experience in life.

The Kingdom of God

When Jesus was in Israel over 2000 years ago, He taught men about true love, righteousness, the spiritual realm, the mercy of God, redemption, the judgement of the world, afterlife and eternal life. His ultimate teaching, however, was about the Kingdom of God; all His other teachings were to prepare His followers for this Kingdom (Matthew 4:17, Mark 1:15). This is relevant to our discussion because, the path of Scripture is the path of Yeshua, the Messiah. In other words, the righteousness that the Bible demands of men is the righteousness of Yeshua (Romans 3:20-21; 10:1-4). According to Scripture, the Kingdom of God is "*righteousness and peace and joy in the Holy [Spirit]*", which also means that it is within a person (in the heart/inner man) (Luke 17:21, Romans 14:17). The kingdom is the domain where God rules; therefore, to be in the kingdom or to have the kingdom in you, means being under the rule of God. God's rule is righteousness, peace and joy; hence, the Bible declares, "*...let the peace of God rule in your hearts...*" (Colossians 3:15). To surrender our hearts to be ruled by the righteousness, joy and peace of Yeshua, is the true meaning of being a follower of Him. We know that there is a physical aspect of this kingdom which Christians are waiting for to be revealed in the time to come. We are not concerned about that part of the kingdom here but with the part that is most relevant to counselling now, which is the part that affects the inner man. Note that the righteousness, peace and joy spoken of here are of divine origin; this is what the phrase "*in the Holy [Spirit]*" indicates. It means that these only come from God and is different from the false sense of peace, joy and self-righteousness practiced by men. It is different in that, it is not affected by the circumstances of life but remains within the person if they continue on the path and under the rule of Jesus (Matthew 5:20, John 14:27, Philippians 4:7).

Now how does one follow Jesus? To follow the path of Jesus means ***1)*** accepting that He is the promised Messiah, Saviour and God of the world ***2)*** believing that He is the one who delivers humanity from Satan, sin, sickness, death and the wrath of God ***3)*** completely submit to Him and obey Him (Isaiah 9:6; 53, Matthew 1:21; 16:24, John 3:16).

The Significance of the Kingdom

Like most other kingdoms, the highlight and glory of the kingdom of heaven is the King himself. He is the centrepiece, glory, wonder and splendour of the Kingdom. It goes without saying that the kingdom gets its significance from Him; because of Him, the kingdom is eternal and full of glory and power (Psalms 145:13, Luke 1:33, 1 Corinthians 4:20). His name Yahweh-Yeshua is translated "I AM-SAVIOUR" which is His most popular name. Let us look however at some of His other names.

Yahweh-Shalom-*The Lord is peace* (Judges 6:24).

El-Deah-God of knowledge. Wisdom comes from the Lord* (1 Samuel 2:3; Romans 11:33-36; 1 Corinthians 1:18-31).

Yahweh-Maccaddeshem-*The Lord your sanctifier. The one who makes holy* (Exodus 31:13, Leviticus 20:8; Ezekiel 37:28).

Yahweh-Rapha-*The Lord our healer (*Exodus 15:26, Exodus 15:26, 2 Chronicles 7:14, Psalm 6:2, 41:4, 103:3, 147:3, Isaiah 19:22, 30:36, 57:18-19, Jeremiah 3:22; 17:14).

Yahweh-Jireh-*The Lord will provide* (Genesis 22:13-14).

El-Roi-*The strong one who sees* (Genesis 16:13).

Yahweh-Shammah-*The Lord who is present. He never leaves you, nor forsakes you.* (Ezekiel 48:35, Genesis 28:15, Ezekiel 48:35, Psalm 23:4, 46:1, 139:7-12, Jeremiah 23:23-24, Amos 5:14).

Yahweh-Nissi-*The Lord our banner. The Lord gives us victory* (Exodus 17:15).

Yahweh-Ghmolah-*The God of Recompense* (Jeremiah 51:6).

El-Chuwl-The God who gave birth. God is our Creator and our Father.* (Psalm 139:13-18).

No other being at any time in the universe has worn all these names or fulfil all these tasks. Clearly, Yahweh-Yeshua is the most significant being in all of existence. As shown by His names, He is the source of life, love, healing, victory, peace, knowledge, wisdom and protection (Deuteronomy 20:4, John 10:10, Colossians 2:3). He is also the source of hope and liberty (2 Corinthians 3:17, Colossians 1:27, Galatians 5:1, 13, Hebrew 6:19). Again, the hope spoken of here is not the wishful thinking and finger crossing of men; rather, it is a living, active hope. In other words, true hope is not an emotion; it is a person, His name is Yeshua (Hebrew 6:19). He is also righteousness, peace, joy, faith and love. Those who possess the kingdom possess Him.

It is now evident that the path of Scripture is the path of Yeshua. Yeshua leads to the kingdom of God, and the kingdom leads to the father and saviour of humanity, who is the personification of righteousness, joy, peace and love. In simple terms, the destination of Scripture is God Himself.

The Synchronicity between counselling and the Bible

Both counsellors and counselees seek wisdom/ knowledge (truth), restoration, love, joy, peace, courage, confidence and security, as the means to enhance well-being. The Bible points to the source of all that humans need for life and godliness (2 Peter 1:3). It contains age old tried and proven principles, practices and instructions that lead to well-being (victory, prosperity and successful living). We can say, what counselling seeks, the Bible offers. We can also say that what counsellors aim to accomplish, God also aims to accomplish; although, the biblical standard is far superior to that of the secular counsellor. The great difference is that, God's well-being program is perfect and complete. He is not experimenting with man or studying him. He knows mankind perfectly well. The Bible shows that God has the welfare of man on His mind. He wants no evil to come to man. His desire is for man to live in victory and prosperity; hence, He sent Jesus to lead and deliver men out of darkness and into His Kingdom, that humanity may be united with Him (Isaiah 61, Jeremiah 29:11, John 3:16, Colossian 1:13,1Timothy 2:3-4, 2 Peter 3:9).

Yeshua's well-being program is called 'Salvation', which simply means 'deliverance' (John 1:29; 3:16, Romans 1:17, 2 Peter 3:9); however, Strong's Dictionary also offers the following synonyms: *welfare, prosperity* and *victory*. God wants to deliver humanity from the power of Satan, sin, sickness, death and His own wrath, so that man may be victorious and prosperous in all areas of life. In summary, the Scripture shows that Yahweh-Yeshua, the source of life, love, truth, peace and joy, is the antidote to every counselling issue (James 1:17). The poor, the orphan, the broken family, the broken-hearted, the confused, the fearful, the vile, angry, sick and insane, can find refuge, hope, healing, solution and deliverance in Him and through His Word. Indeed, Yahweh-Yeshua Himself is well-being. Those who find him, find well-being.

Conclusion

What has been covered in this book is merely the scope of Scripture; however, further study on the depth of Scripture would be far more beneficial to the counsellor. Note however, the Bible must not be treated as a mere textbook; it is a holy, living, spiritual book. It should be practiced with reverence and not just studied. When we consider the track record and the positive effect the Bible has on our world, we cannot deny that it stands in a class by itself. It contains a wealth of knowledge that is authoritative, extensive and relevant to counselling. Its presentation of anthropology, psychology and sociology has stood the test of time, never needing updates or revisions. Its variety of topics and depth of wisdom is vast enough to make a counsellor competent in identifying and solving emotional, psychological, spiritual, behavioural and relational problems. This makes the Bible superior to any other school of thought, source of knowledge and voice of authority. Indeed, the Bible is tried and proven. It is the perfect source of solutions for both counsellor and counselee (Psalm 19:7).

Where do we go from here?

As helpers and counsellors, we must be honest with ourselves and admit that the efforts of man have not produced anything superior to the Holy Bible to help us understand and fix the complexities of humanity. We must be careful then not to sacrifice the souls of men on the altar of scientific advancement and humanistic philosophies. Man is the image of God; therefore, we must guard against the temptation to treat humans like lab rats. Human life is precious and sacred, and it must be treated with utmost respect. When we approach the human soul, we must do so only in the authority of its Creator. When we address his problems, we must do so according to the laws of his King, and when we touch his wounds, we must do so with the love of his Father.

I hereby charge secular counsellors to lay down their theories and speculations for the perfect truth and the perfect way of Yahweh-Yeshua. His healing, counselling and deliverance ministry has a perfect track record which has stood the test of time. I charge the Christian worker to stand firm in the calling of God; not to be tossed to and fro by every wind of doctrine or philosophy. Let not your confidence be in much knowledge and many books but in the blood, spirit, name and power of Yeshua, the Messiah and Saviour.

"Not that we are sufficient of ourselves to think any thing as of ourselves; but our sufficiency is of God" (2 Corinthian 3:5).

Appendix

Some other topics covered in the Bible

The human body: Its origin, purpose, future, healthcare, sleep, food, sickness and Death etc. (Genesis 1:29; 2:7; 9:3-4, Proverbs 3:7-8; 17:22, Matthew 6:22-23, Acts 27:34, I Corinthians 6:19-20, James 3:6).

Leadership/management: Integrity, responsibility, administration, organisation, motivation, business/finances, rulemaking, conflict management, military engagements etc. (Exodus 18:21, Joshua 7-9, Psalms 32:8; 78:72, Proverbs 12:18; 27:23-24, Matthew 5-7; 18:15-17, Luke 6:31, Philippians 2:3).

Sexuality: Sexual orientation, prostitution, sex in marriage (Mark 10:6-9, Romans 1:26-28, 1 Corinthians 6:15-16; 7:1-14, 1 Timothy 1:8-11, Hebrews 13:4).

Witchcraft/Sorcery: Divination, Necromancy, drug use (Exodus 7:11, Leviticus 19:31; 20:6, Isaiah 8:19, Acts 16:16, Revelation 18:23; 21:8).

Afterlife: heaven, hell, reward, judgment, eternity (Isaiah 5:14, Psalm 49:9, Proverbs 23:14, Matthew 22:23-31, Mark 10:30, John 6:33, 1 Corinthians 15, Revelation 6:8).

Wisdom for daily living: Book of Psalms, Proverbs and Ecclesiastes.

In summary, the Bible contains God's self-disclosure, God's salvation plan, God's wisdom, God's truth, God's perspective on man, His laws, promises and plan for the future of the universe.

About the Author

Rev. Jermaine Jerome James is an ordained pastor, chaplain and trained counsellor, holding a bachelor's degree in Christian Counselling, a Master of Divinity and an Order of Pastoral Counsellor. He has spent many years in mental health and spiritual counselling with individuals and families; specializing in youth counselling, this includes work in the deliverance ministry (casting out of demons). Jermaine currently works as a Counsellor in the Canadian youth justice system while he continues to practice in his own private counselling ministry. Jermaine lives with his wife Victoria and their three children in Brampton, Ontario, Canada.

Other Book: ***7 Powers of Man***

References

Adams, J. (1970). *Competent to counsel*. Grand Rapids, Michigan: Zandervan

Adams, J. (1973). *The Christian counselor's manual*. Grand Rapids, Michigan: Zandervan

Adams, J. (1974). The use of the Scriptures in counseling part 1: Christian counseling is scriptural. *Bibliotheca Sacra* / Vol 131:521 (Jan 1974)

Adams, J. (1974). The use of the Scripture in counseling part IV: *Scriptural counseling is spiritual. Bibliotheca Sacra* / Vol 131:524 (Oct 1974)

Ancient Hebrew Research Center. www.ancient-hebrew.org/

Arp, W. (1997). All grace and grace alone. *Reformation and Revival Journal* / Vol 06:10 (Fall 1997)

Aucamp, A. (2013). A systematic approach to God's attributes. *Conspectus* / Vol 15:1 (March 2013)

Austin, T. (1995). The glory of God. *Reformation and Revival Journal* / Vol 04:2 (Spring 1995)

Boccia, M. L. (2011). Human interpersonal relationships and the love of the trinity. *Priscilla Papers* / Vol 25:4 (autumn 2011)

Bogosh, C. (2009). Pastoral counseling in the twenty first century for illness, disease and death. *Puritan Reformed Journal* / Vol 01:1 (Jan 2009)

Boyd, J.H. (1996). An insider's effort to blow up psychiatry. *Trinity Journal* / Vol 17:2 (Fall 1996)

Boyd, L.H. (1997). One's self-concept and biblical theology. *Journal of the Evangelical Theological Society* / Vol 40:2 (Jun 1997)

Brackman, L. (2008, May 09). Why Jews are disproportionally successful. Retrieved from ynet: https://www.ynetnews.com/articles/0,7340,L-3592566,00.html

Buswell III, J.O (1970). Anthropology and the nature of man. *Journal of the Evangelical Theological Society* / Vol 13:4 (Fall 1970*)*

Catanzaro III, F.J. (2000). Why biblical counsel? *Faith and Mission Journal* / Vol 17:2 (Spring 2000)

Chafer, L.S. (1943). Anthropology part 1. *Bibliotheca Sacra* / Vol 100:398 (April 1943)

Churchill, H. (1900). Religion as a personal Relation. *Bibliotheca Sacra* / Vol 057:227 (Jul 1900)

Cochran, G.C. (2011). Remembering the father in fatherhood: Biblical foundations and practical implications of the doctrine of the fatherhood of God. *Journal of Discipleship and Family Ministry/* Vol 01:2 (spring 2011)

Conner, K. J. (1990). *The foundations of Christian Doctrine.* Portland, Oregon: City Bible publishing

Constantineanu, C. (2010). The authority of Scripture as the word of God. *KAIROS - Evangelical Journal of Theology* / Vol. IV. No. 1 (2010), pp. 13-2

Counseling psychology *(2018). APA, http://www.apa.org/ed/graduate/specialize/counseling.aspx*

Cook, C. (2018). *https://www.crossmap.com/blogs/is-christian-counseling-effective-what-the-research-shows.html*. Retrieved from https://www.crossmap.com: https://www.crossmap.com

Darby, J.N. (1995). A voice from the past: The true grace of God on which you stand. *Journal of the Grace Evangelical Society* / Vol 08:2 (autumn 1995)

Dixon, L. (2000). What Is Man.? *Emmaus Journal* / 09:2 (Winter 2000)

Due, N. (2004). Pastoral counseling: Biblical foundations and framework. *Reformation and Revival Journal* / Vol 13:2 (Spring 2004)

Duncan, L. (2004). A call to family worship. *Journal for Biblical Manhood and Womanhood* / Vol 09:1 (spring 2004)

Elwell, A. W. (1996). *Baker's Evangelical Dictionary of Biblical Theology* (online version). Grand Rapids, Michigan: Baker books

Epilepsy Ontario 2018. http://epilepsyontario.org/about-epilepsy/causes/

Epilepsy Society facts / Epilepsy Society 2018. Retrieved from

https://www.epilepsysociety.org.uk/epilepsy-society-facts#.WqAU12rwbct

Evans, J.E. (1960). The Christian approach of counseling. *Bibliotheca Sacra* / Vol 117:468 (Oct 1960)

Fairchild, J. H. (1884). The divine personality. *Bibliotheca Sacra* / Vol 041:162 (Apr 1884)

Fairchild, J. H. (1868). The Nature of Sin. *Bibliotheca Sacra* / Vol 025:97 (Jan 1868)

Firmin, M.W. & Becknell, M.E. (2008). A Christian perspective of health. *Journal of Ministry and Theology* / Vol 12:2 (Fall 2008)

Green, W. S. & Neusner, J. (2002). *Dictionary of Judaism in the biblical period.* Peabody, Massachusetts Hendrickson publishers 2002,

Good News Bible © 1994. USA. HarperCollins

Gonzales, R. Jr. (2008). Man's constitution as a physical-spiritual unity. *Journal of Reformed Baptist Theological Review* / 06:1 (Jan 2009)

Gonzales, R. Jr. (2008). Man: God's visible replica and vice-regent. *Journal of Reformed Baptist Theological Review* / Vol 05:2 (Jul 2008)

Grabmeier, J. (2009). Family stability may be more crucial than two parents for child success. *phys.org. Retrieved from https://phys.org/news/2009-08-family-stability-crucial-parents-child.html*

Grata, C.T. (2002). Our heavenly father. *Emmaus Journal* / Vol 11:2 (winter 2002)

Grenz, S.J. (2004). Jesus as the imago dei: Image-of-God Christology and the non-linear linearity of theology. *Journal of the Evangelical Theological Society* / Vol 47:4 (Dec 2004)

Hempy, R.P. Jr. (1998). The sufficiency of Scripture and modern psychology. *Chafer Theological Seminary Journal* / Vol 04:1 (Jan 1998)

Henry, J.F. (2008). Man in God's image: "What Does It Mean?" *Journal of Dispensational Theology* / Vol 12:37 (Dec 2008)

Hill, J. (1905). A plea for the family. *Bibliotheca Sacra* / Vol 062:248 (Oct 1905)

Hinson, E. E. (1982). The inerrancy debate and the use of Scripture in counseling. *Grace Theological Journal* / Vol 03:2 (Fall 1982)

Hodge, C. *Systematic theology vol. 2*. Grand Rapids, Michigan: Wm. B. Eerdmans Publishing Company

Horne, C.M. (1971). Christain Humanism. *Journal of the Evangelical Theological Society* / Vol 14:3 (summer 1971)

House, P.R. (1997). Theology transforming culture. *Southern Baptist Journal of Theology* / Vol 01:2 (Summer 1997)

Johnson, E.L. (2003). How God is good for the soul. *Southern Baptist Journal of Theology* / Vol 07:4 (Winter 2003)

Kassian, M.A (2000). Father of the fatherless. *Journal for Biblical Manhood and Womanhood* / Vol 04:4 (spring 2000)

Kendler, K.S. (2005). "Toward a philosophical structure for psychiatry", *American Journal of Psychiatry* / Vol 162: 433–440, 2005.

Lambert, H. (2012). The gospel and mental illness. *ISBN-13*

Lacasse, J.R. & Gomory, T. (2003). "Is graduate social work education promoting a critical approach to mental health practice?" *Journal of Social Work Education* / Vol 39: 383–408, 2003

Lemke, S.W (2003). Evangelical theology in the thirty first century. *Journal for Baptist Theology and Ministry* / Vol 01:1 (spring 2003)

Lewis, A.W. (1929). God's love is saving the world. *Bibliotheca Sacra* / Vol 086:343 (Jul 1929)

Lucas, R. C. (1994). The grace of God. *Reformation and Revival Journal* / Vol 03:1 (winter 1994)

Mears, H. C. (2011). In What the Bible is all About. Ventura: Regal.

MacArthur, J. F. Jr. (1991). The psychology, epidemic and its cure. *Masters Seminary Journal* / Vol 02:1 (spring 1991)

MacArthur, J. F. Jr. (2004). The sufficiency of Scriptures. *The Master's Seminary Journal* / Vol 15:2 (Fall 2004)

MacILvaine III, W. R. & Stewart, W. C. (2013). The apologetic value of religion and wellness studies. *Christain Apologetic Journal* / Vol 11:1 (spring 2013)

Mack, W.A. (1998). The sufficiency of Scripture in counseling. *The Master's Seminary Journal* / Vol 9/1 (Spring 1998)

Makujina, J. (1997). The second greatest commandment and self-esteem. *Masters Seminary Journal* / Vol 08:2 (Fall 1997)

Mayhue, R. L. (2004). The authority of Scripture. *The Master's Seminary Journal* / Vol 16/2 (Fall 2004)

Merriam Webster. Retrieved from https://www.merriam-webster.com

Merrins, E. M. (1904). The malady of Saul, king of Israel. *Bibliotheca Sacra* / Vol 061:244 (Oct 1904)

Meyer, V. (1985). God is love. *Ashland Theological Journal* / Vol 18:0 (NA 1985)

McConnell, W.T. (1927). The social teachings of our Lord. *Bibliotheca Sacra* / Vol 084:333 (Jan 1927)

Mcgoldrick, J.E. (1998). The Christlikeness of God. *Reformation and Revival Journal* / Vol 07:2 (Spring 1998)

Mcquilkin, J.R. (1977). The Behavioral sciences under the authority of Scripture. *Journal of the Evangelical Theological Society* / Vol 20:1 (winter 1977)

Murray, D. P (2014). A theology of sleep. *Puritan Reformed Journal* / Vol 06:2 (Jul 2014)

Nichols, L.M. & Hunt, B. (2011). The significance of spirituality for individuals with chronic illness: Implications for mental health counseling. *Journal of Mental Health Counseling* / Vol 33/1 (January 2018)

Ouweneel, W. J. (2014). *Wisdom for thinkers*. Ontario, Canada: Paideia press

Oxford living dictionary (online). *Retrieved from*

https://en.oxforddictionaries.com/definition/online

Pendleton, J. M. (1878). *Christmas doctrine.* Upland P.A: The Judson Press

Powlison, D. (2005). The sufficiency of Scripture to diagnose and cure souls. *The Journal of Biblical Counseling,* Spring 2005

Ramsay, S. W. (1953). The bearing of recent discoveries on the trustworthiness of the New Testament. *Grand Rapids, MI: Baker Book House*

Richardson, A. *A theological word book of the bible.* New York, New York 10022: MacMillan Publishing

Ross, H. (2013). Retrieved from http://www.reasons.org/articles/articles/fulfilled-prophecy-evidence-for-the-reliability-of-the-bible

Rosenberg, M. (2017, September 20). Most Popular Religions. Retrieved from thoughtco: https://www.thoughtco.com/most-popular-world-religions-1434513

Schaeffer, F.A. (1971). He is there and he is not silent part 1: Philosophy's metaphysical problem as answered in the existence of the infinite-personal, Triune God. *Bibliotheca Sacra* / Vol 128:510 (Apr 1971)

Scipione, G. (1974). The wonderful counselor, the other counselor and the christain counselor. *Westminster Theological Journal* / Vol 36:2 (Winter 1974)

Sheppard, G. Notebook on Ethics, Legal issues and Standards for Counsellors: "What is counseling" *Retrieved from https://www.ccpa-accp.ca/*

Simmons, N.G.S. (2009). The Religiosity of American College and University Professors. *Sociology of Religion* /Vol 70, Issue 2, 1 July 2009, Pages 101–129, https://doi.org/10.1093/socrel/srp026

Smalley, E. (1850). Theology of Dr. Emmons. *Bibliotheca Sacra /* Vol 007:26 (Apr 1850)

Stevenson, A & Lindberg, C. A. (2015). *New Oxford American dictionary (third edition).* Oxford University Press

Straucha, A. (2003). The trinity and doctrine of Love. *Emmaus Journal /* Vol 12:2 (Winter 2003)

Strong, J. (2015). *Strong's Dictionary.* Best Books

Swenson, C. C, Saldana, S. (2007). *Child abuse.* Medical university of South Carolina Charleston, SC, USA: *ELSEVIER*

Tautges, P. (2013). www.counselingoneanother.com

Turbott, J. (2004). Treatment of borderline personality disorder. *Australian Psychiatry /* Vol 12:3, doi: 10.1111/j.1039-8562.2004.02103.x-i2

Unger, M.F. (1957). The Old Testament revelation of the beginning of sin. *Bibliotheca Sacra /* Vol 114:456 (Oct 1957)

Unger, M. F. (1980). *Unger's Bible dictionary.* Chicago: Moody press

Valenstein, E. (1988). Blaming the brain: The truth about drugs and mental health, *Free Press, New York*, 1988

Verghese, A. (2008). Spirituality and mental health. *Indian Journal of psychiatry /* Vol 50(4) Oct-Dec 2008

Vines, W. E, Unger, M. & White, W. (1984). *Vines complete expository dictionary.* Nashville, TN Thomas Nelson Publishers

Wagner-Harper, M. E. (1975). *The sensation of being somebody.* New York, New York

Ward, J.W. (1845). The authority of God. *Bibliotheca Sacra /* Vol 002:7 (Aug 1845)

Watson, J.F. (1985). A contemporary model: Jesus as friend. *Ashland Theological Journal* / Vol 18:0 (NA 1985

Wood, S. E, Wood, E. G, Boyd. D, Wood, E & Desmarais, S. (2014). *The world of Psychology 7th edition* Pearson Canada Inc, Toronto, Ontario

Wellum, S.J (2013). Editorial: Reflections of living in light of sin and evil. *Southern Baptist Journal of Theology* / Vol 17:4 (Winter 2013)

Wright, W. E. C. (1901). Sociology a psychological study. *Bibliotheca Sacra* / Vol 058:230 (Apr 1901)

Made in the USA
Monee, IL
04 November 2026

67387183R00085